THE ARCHITECTURE AND LANDSCAPE ARCHITECTURE OF JONES & JONES

LIVING PLACES

BY CLAIR ENLOW

Spacemaker

THE ARCHITECTURE AND LANDSCAPE ARCHITECTURE OF JONES & JONES

LIVING PLACES

BY CLAIR ENLOW

The Architecture and Landscape Architecture of Jones & Jones
Living Places
By Clair Enlow

PUBLISHER
Spacemaker Press, LLC
James G. Trulove, Publisher
1250 28th Street, NW
Washington, DC 20007
202-337-1380

DESIGN
James Pittman

FONT
Priori Serf

ISBN 0-9749632-4-0

Printed in China

First printing, 2006

1 2 3 4 5 6 7 8 9 / 09 08 07 06

Acknowledgements

I would like to acknowledge Grant Jones, Ilze Jones, and Johnpaul Jones. With their evolving, activist practice, they continue to demonstrate what it means for designers to engage with the world. Their leadership inspires this book. They continue to attract and develop talented people who, like themselves, will not be confined by professional labels and who demand that design be relevant and responsible to future generations.

Special thanks to principals Mario Campos and Keith Larson, who provided important input, to Kevin Carl, who was a steward for the project, and to Pamela Shields, who put in countless hours keeping this book on track. I would also like to thank Nate Cormier, Colleen Thorpe, Bruce Arnold, Mark Johnson, Paul Olson, and Charlie Scott. Their intimate familiarity with some very complex projects—and the many creative decisions that went into them—were critical in writing about the work of Jones & Jones.

—Clair Enlow

CONTENTS

INTRODUCTION
CLAIR ENLOW

Deep in the foothills of the Cascade Mountains, the new education campus for the Cedar River watershed seems curiously settled, arranged by forces of nature or tradition. The buildings are clearly of this age. Yet they belong, as if they had always been here—like the water. In a way, this project has been here as long as the water. The center belongs to the city of Seattle, but water is the real client. From the peaks of the steep roofs to the planted covers over the walkways, to the moss gardens and the runnels, the rain is welcomed, heard, and released. The message is water conservation, for salmon and people. Rain, river, buildings, art, land and landscape—they all speak together here, along with the visiting children. The quieter voices sing, and the real world beneath the surface is realized. A multi-disciplinary design firm called Jones & Jones Architects and Landscape Architects is only one of the voices. This is not so much a project as it is a continuing dialog. It can't be easily classified as architecture, landscape architecture, or any other name in the professional world. It's simply there, enfolding the visitor along with the sound of the drumming rain.

In the Cedar River watershed and everywhere on earth, the spirit of place contains infinite possibility and profound paradox. It's found in geologic time and layers of historic material. It crosses boundaries, goes beyond science, and involves all the senses. It is unique to a location, yet expressive of the world. When a project is place-based, all aspects of the built environment are naturally subsumed in the spirit and idea of the landscape.

Jones & Jones has helped to create a language of place, reaching beyond the traditional boundaries of the architecture and landscape architecture professions, and bringing other disciplines inside the circle. Principals Ilze Jones, Grant Jones, Johnpaul Jones, Keith Larson, Mario Campos, and Chris Overdorf—and all who have contributed to their firm—have mixed science and art in a unique practice. So far, the process has taken place in zoos and botanical gardens, rivers, roads, and urban places from Singapore to Seattle and Washington, D.C., to Jerusalem. In each of these areas of practice, the firm has changed the way a project type is addressed.

In zoo design, Jones & Jones pioneered the concept of landscape bioimmersion, bringing visitors into a species-specific animal habitat based on conditions in the wild. The firm also developed a language for analyzing the aesthetic resources in large geographic areas, a language that allows decision-makers to account, as never before, for the advantages and costs of development decisions. In Seattle and other cities, Jones & Jones has brought oxygen into neglected streets and squares, brushing off the pavings of the past and anticipating the future with art works and new plantings. Following in this tradition, precedent-setting highway projects have shifted the center of transportation planning away from two-dimensional traffic engineering and toward communities and respect for the land. As activists in their home base of Seattle, the firm's founders are challenging city and state planners to combine urban waterfront planning with renewed shoreline habitat.

The world has noticed. The work of Jones & Jones has been recognized with over 100 awards, and the list is a testament to the firm's influence in a wide range of professional specialties, from architecture and landscape architecture to environmental preservation and transportation planning. In 2003, Jones & Jones received the first-ever Firm Award from the American Society of Landscape Architects.

Founders Grant and Ilze tell a story from their days as students together at the University of Washington. It was before they made history: before the first gorilla emerged into the sun from his tiled cell at the Woodland Park Zoo, before landscape architects created road modeling programs so they could redesign highways, and before Native Americans began to celebrate the solstice in their own cultural center on the National Mall. In protest against the planned installation of fluorescent lights in their work space, the pair set up a squatters' studio with their compatriots in the abundant natural light on the top floor of the architecture department. Most of the faculty ignored them. Their mentor, Richard Haag, did not. He recognized the philosophical scope of their protest. Borrowing the famous title from playwright Samuel Beckett, he asked, "What are you doing? Waiting for Godot?"—and shooed them out of their makeshift digs and on to Cambridge, Mass., for professional practice and graduate school at Harvard.

Just as Grant and Ilze took a stand as students against the harsh artificial light in their environment, they are still taking stands against the environmental abuses of modernism and market economics, the "progress" that destroys the heart of cities, leaves small communities faceless, and cuts precious habitat into fragments. Theirs is a creative struggle against market-based development that renders only placeless homogeneity and degraded land. Perhaps most significantly, the work of Jones & Jones stands as a contrast to an international design culture that celebrates itself at the expense of real, live neighborhoods, place-based home-grown cultures, and environmental health. In his poetic writings about practice, Grant has said that "architects and landscape architects, like other artists, are either earth-connected or market-connected."

The culture of Jones & Jones has been called "tribal." As if on a quest, the founding principals have always reached for the hard problem, the long view, and the holistic vision. Together, the extended tribe has shifted and blurred the boundaries between traditional design disciplines as they frame a new problem or redefine a traditional one in the landscape.

Johnpaul, also a founding principal, has built an integrated philosophy of architecture grounded in his Native American heritage and based on organic connections between buildings, land, and inhabitants, and between the four worlds of spirit, nature, animals, and humans.

Forever seeking out projects with unique issues and unprecedented possibilities, the three founders have been joined by three more principals. Keith Larson manages complex, multidisciplinary zoo and park projects. He has used the planning reputation and environmental focus of the firm to build relationships with the National Park Service and make important technical and technological strides in the field of zoo design. Mario Campos helps shape cultural, educational, and recreational facilities and leads community planning efforts. Reaching out to communities and neighborhoods, non-profits, and minority groups with a participatory design approach, he has built on the tribal traditions of the firm and brought a new multi-cultural facet to Jones & Jones. Chris Overdorf adds broad expertise in digital technology and planning.

Together they enable clients to move beyond narrow goals and old conflicts to reach for a fuller sense of time and possibility. As they do this, they provide hope that the world can move from short-term exploitation of resources toward respect for the earth and balance with nature.

As Ilze has said, "Evolution doesn't just happen—it happens because individuals take risks and define their future by creating their future."

Over the last three decades, many places have been touched or interpreted by Jones & Jones. In the process, they've evolved—gaining memory, visibility, and a foundation for future generations. The work reminds us that we are all intimately connected to each other, to our own history, and to other species. By learning from the land, Jones & Jones claims and celebrates that connection—before it slips even further away from all of us.

CEDAR RIVER WATERSHED EDUCATION CENTER
NORTH BEND, WASHINGTON
1999

Pristine, protected slopes make the Cedar River watershed one of the only municipal water sources in the United States that needs no filtration. Closed to the public, more than 90,000 acres of the upper river basin has been designated as an ecological reserve. The basin contains 14,000 acres of old growth forest, providing critical wildlife habitat for elk, spotted owls, cougar, bull trout, and the largest run of sockeye salmon in the Northwest.

The city of Seattle is connected by an umbilical pipeline to the Cedar River, a reliable source of clean water for more than a century. Building the pipeline was a bold project, and protecting the source in the modern era is a political challenge. But in this challenge is a lesson with world-wide implications: The goal of protecting water cannot be separated from the need to preserve natural ecosystems and habitat.

The Cedar River Watershed Education Center will help future generations understand the special nature of the place. School groups and drop-in visitors circulate through the center, into its laboratories, and out into its surrounding grounds. Others come to participate in special events such as teacher training sessions, receptions, and tribal gatherings.

The five-acre building and landscape complex is located in the Cascade foothills near North Bend, which receives well over 60 inches of precipitation a year. Here, falling rain is caught, put into play, and celebrated. Courtyards and interior spaces are threaded together with a narrative of water. A naturalistic stream begins in a spring and travels in a progression of rivulets and marshes through the complex. The stream collects the surface drainage as well as the roof waters that are allowed to drop their full height from the broad building eaves.

The Cedar River Watershed is the primary source of drinking water for Seattle. Ninety thousand acres of the upper river basin, managed by Seattle Public Utilities, has been designated as an ecological reserve.

Once an overused lakefront and log yard, Rattlesnake Lake Park is ecologically enhanced and better organized for recreational use in harmony with the beauty and presence of Rattlesnake Ledge.

The water itself speaks most audibly to visitors in the forested center courtyard, a reconstructed lowland-Cascades woodland partially edged by the stream. Vine maples surround a deeply layered moss garden. Arranged in free-form composition, a collection of rain drums created by the project artist amplifies the sounds of raindrops. Charged by collected rainwater, an intricate system of tubing laced through the trees plays world rhythms via water droplets discharged through computer-controlled emitters.

From the courtyard, the stream flows under the building. It emerges on the other side as a native-boulder-lined pool in front of arriving visitors in the entry court, a gathering and orientation space with low stone bench walls and an information kiosk.

Water is slowed and filtered throughout the complex. Steep metal roofs with gushing sheets of water lead to sod roofs, where the water seeps slowly through the thicket of plant covering. Roof gutters feed the stream, and falling water is caught in boulder basins. Drainage from the parking lots is channeled into bioswales planted with wetland shrubs that slow and clean the water before it reaches the lake.

Five buildings are linked by a series of courtyards, and interior spaces open to specialized outdoor rooms to provide a variety of settings for meeting, teaching, and discovery. With a floor space of 9,800 square feet, the Cedar River Watershed Education Center includes an interpretive hall with a welcoming room, an auditorium, classrooms, a library, offices, and archive storage areas. Post and beam construction, wood siding, stone foundations, and sheltering roof overhangs are meant to evoke historic settlement on the site.

Permanent exhibits inside the center interpret the history and habitats of the watershed and show the workings and management of the water system from reservoir to river to drinking fountain. Staff teachers and visitors can use these to tell the story of how water is captured and treated.

Auditorium and classroom buildings open to a secondary courtyard with cues to the cultural heritage of the place. With paving that includes historic clay tile artifacts from the watershed, the courtyard evokes the former town site, which is still partially visible across the lake.

Natural and human history determined the overall shape of the education center. The site was selected for ease of access at the edge of the protected basin, and the campus is laid out along a narrow ridgeline that follows the historic Milwaukee Railroad corridor and overlooks Rattlesnake Lake. It is organized around a linear walkway, which is aligned with an existing allee of 80-year-old big leaf maples planted on top of the ridgeline. The walkway connects the main buildings and small supporting structures and situates the campus among traces of old settlements once connected to the railroad. From the Cedar River Watershed Education Center, visitors can enjoy the view of the lake and the dramatic landform of Rattlesnake Ledge above.

At the Cedar River Watershed Education Center, the mission of watershed preservation is combined with the city's overall mission of conservation. The complex is designed to demonstrate principles of ecologically sustainable design. Materials for site and buildings were selected for durability, longevity, and fit with the natural landscape. All wood for the project was specified re-used, or sourced from certified

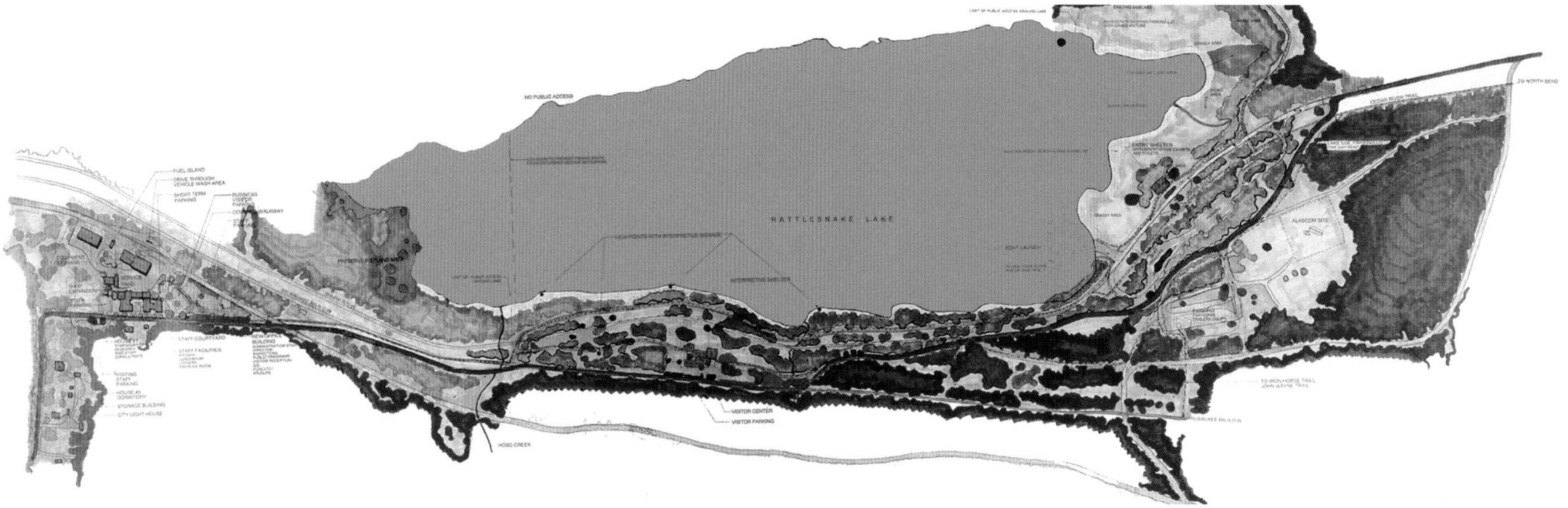

The Education Center was sited as part of master planning for the entire headquarters area, including trail development and ecological restoration of the shoreline and park at Rattlesnake Lake.

well-managed forests. Much of the natural stone in the landscape was collected locally. Soils have a high proportion of compost. Only native plants found in the various habitat areas of the watershed were specified, and small areas devoted to drought-tolerant plants serve as examples for residential water-wise gardening.

Along with protecting the watershed, recreation has its place. Hand in hand with the education center, a master plan provides for the construction of new parking and circulation routes for visitors to Rattlesnake Lake Recreation Area. The lake is an attraction that resulted from accidental seepage when engineers first dammed the river to build the city water system. Now roadway and parking are moved away from the restored shoreline and new picnic areas introduced to remake it as a resting stop for a regional trail system that connects with the Cedar River Watershed Education Center.

The Cedar River pipeline was a feat of engineering. But the Cedar River Watershed Education Center is a triumph of awareness, claiming the consciousness and support of future generations.

Jones & Jones was master planner, architect, and landscape architect for the Cedar River Watershed Education Center for the City of Seattle.

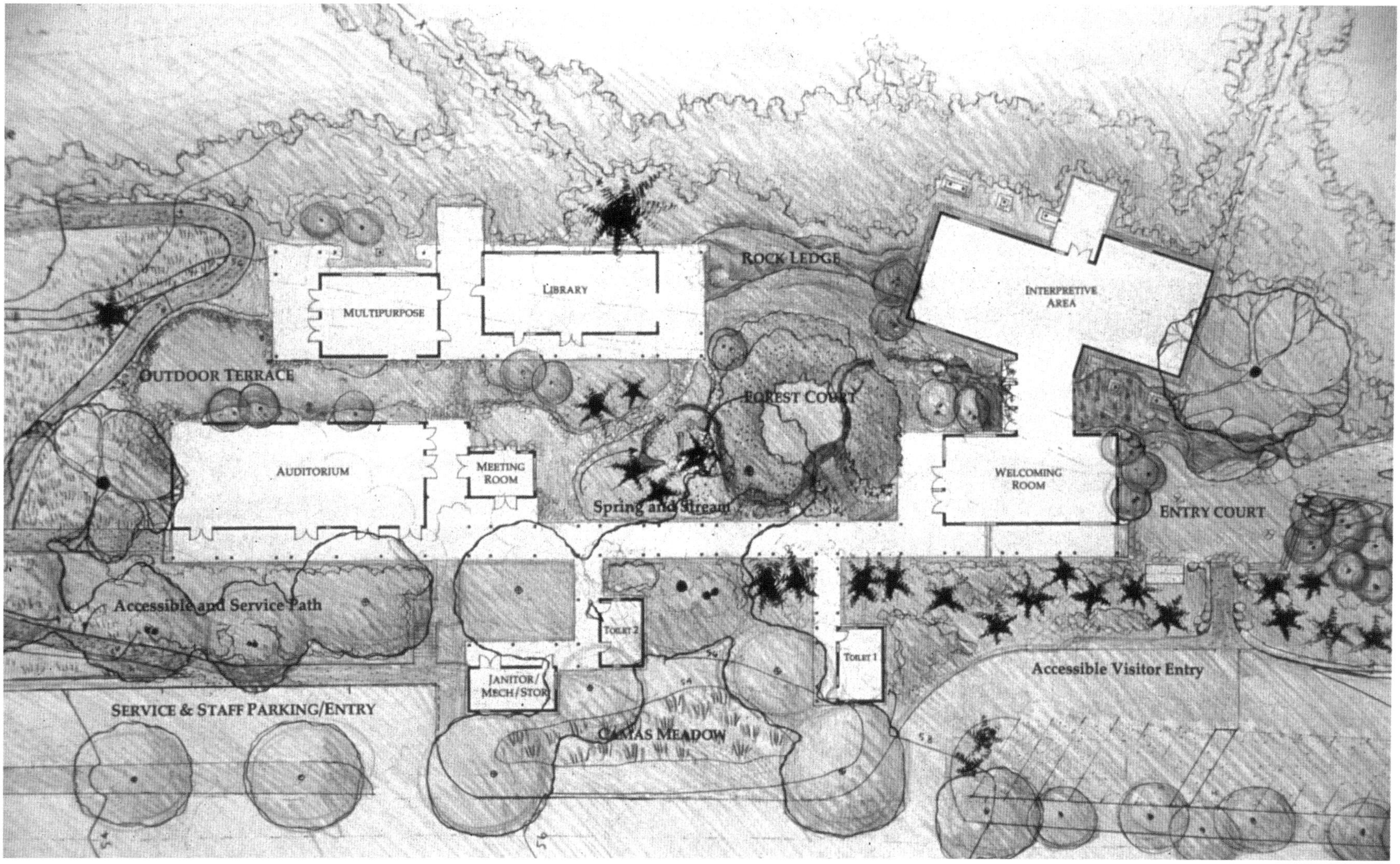

The integrated campus features a series of outdoor courts threaded together by water courses and pathways. The linear layout follows the historic railroad alignment to take advantage of the lake and the mountain views.

LEFT: An expanded rustic park was part of the first design phase, which included visitor amenities such as this orientation kiosk. The kiosk roof was seeded with the same native wildflower mix as the parkland meadows.

BELOW: The campus features several small-scaled wood and stone buildings that shape a series of outdoor courtyards and viewpoints designed to closely integrate the buildings and landscape.

RIGHT: The center of the Forest Court is emblematic of a forest glade, featuring a moss garden that is circumscribed by a marshy stream, a loose ring of vine maples and native ferns, and "rain drums" on which drops of water play world rhythms.

BELOW RIGHT: The forms and material of the Center recall historical structures, and the stone, plants, and water reflect the surrounding landscape.

LEFT: Buildings are connected by a living-roofed boardwalk that parallels the former railway corridor and aligns with an allee of historic big leaf maples, remnants from a turn-of-the-century railroad community.

ABOVE: Native species were used exclusively in the restorative planting of the site.

LEFT: Visitors are welcomed inside with literal and figurative references to the surrounding stories of nature and culture. Embedded art abstracts principles of nature and mirrors them back in delightful and compelling ways.

TOP: Meeting spaces provide views to the light-filled courtyard.

ABOVE: Cubbies, a fire, interpretive art, and parlor furniture welcome school groups, families, and others inside after an entry immersion into the simulated landscape of the watershed.

RIGHT: Providing a much-needed local gathering place, the Center knits together a dispersed rural community with flexible meeting and event spaces. The setting is conducive to inspired decision-making at meetings and retreats for non-profits and businesses.

LEFT: The stream flows under the enclosed bridge and drops over a weir into the pool, providing a constant sound of water in the entry court.

RIGHT: Low landscape lighting washes the ground and vegetation, using minimum light levels to preserve the darkness of the sky. Buildings function as lanterns.

COMMONS PARK

DENVER, COLORADO

2003

Commons Park is the green heart of Denver's future. It's also a historic place-holder in the city, recapturing the grassy expanses of the prairie and the spirit of its original inhabitants. With its network of new trails and vantage points, Commons Park is now the hub of Denver's park system, anchoring a 10.5-mile greenway along the banks of the South Platte River.

This 26-acre park redefines the relationship between human settlement and the river, rebalancing the two so that the city gives more to the river system—and receives more in return. First, the natural and visual presence of the stream is reestablished and enlarged. To this end, formal design and riverine habitat restoration are one and the same. While it recaptures the natural architecture of the river shore, Commons Park also serves as a major city park, with open spaces for recreation, public restrooms, accessible frontage, and river crossing.

Commons Park is the culmination of a master plan decades in the making, a plan designed to refocus development toward a city center served by mass transit and to bring a new wave of residents into the city. It is tied to Denver's rediscovered and rebuilt historic core through a multi-block transit mall and flanked by 21 blocks of new neighborhood development that includes hundreds of new residential units.

The location of the park is known as the birthplace of Denver. Here, the Overland and the Cimmaron trails converged at an Arapaho trading ground. Ironically, the land was designated as a park over a century ago. But the Burlington Northern Railroad and industrial development in the Platte Valley displaced the dream, turning the land into a rail yard and warehouse district. In the meantime, the river itself was dredged and tamed. The natural seepage that would have fed the stream was replaced by the extreme fluctuations of urban runoff.

The Arapaho chief, Little Raven, is honored in the name of a new street that defines the upland edge of the park. But it is the natural heritage of the place that inspired the landscape at the river's edge.

The park lies just downstream from the mouth of Cherry Creek, an important tributary of the South Platte River. Across from Commons

View of the Bridge Plaza overlook with its shade trellis structure.

Park, the widened river meets the bedrock of the Front Range of the Rockies. There, it naturally turns and braids on the flat of the prairie, cutting through sand drifts built up over eons as wind meets rock. Rivulets of rainwater carved the sand into a series of finger-like sandhills and green prairie sloughs along the near shore of the site.

Commons Park reintroduces the sandhill sloughs, and they form a thick, hard-working edge for the park. Diked and armored banks were laid back and sandhills mounded higher. The undulating shoreline now supports native riparian plants. The streamway itself is widened and recarved into a more naturally sinuous course. The water is interrupted and slowed with riverbed sills and side jetties, which result in more sand deposits and holes on the bottom, for greater range of habitat.

In the sloughs, the natural hydrology of the prairie is reinterpreted and reinstated. Storm runoff from the grid of new nearby streets is caught at the perimeter and channeled underneath the landscape, emerging to seep in small rivulets through the marsh swales and into the river. The same runoff, pre-cleaned by sand filters, also rises to the surface in a new wetland created on site. Bulrushes and cattails, sedges, and Indian grass have all been reinstated in the wetlands. Moving upland, there are chokecherries, cottonwoods, juniper, and pines.

While it points to a sustainable future for the city, Commons Park also expands on the best traditions of 19th Century park design, with broad grassy expanses, soft green borders, dramatic vantage points, and substantial architectural features.

For the visitor, the park is largely defined by two unique architectural elements: a stone-clad restroom building positioned near the transit mall gateway to the park shares a vocabulary of stone and steel with a prominent outlook near the river bank.

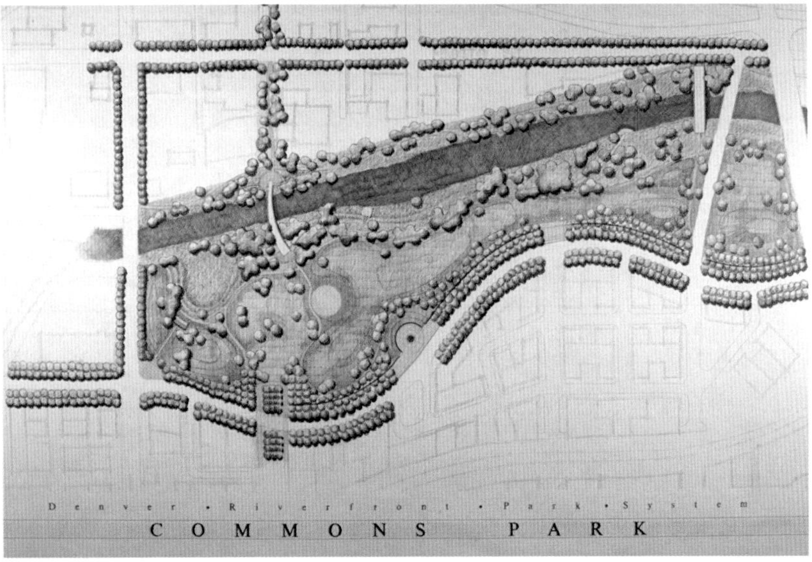

Commons Park illustrative plan.

Flowing in plan, each of these structures is dominated by a large, serpentine-edged steel trellis and based on massive platforms with retaining walls built from buff-colored Colorado Lyon's sandstone. Each trellis is a collage of stacked and overlapping steel grids which shade visitors from the prairie sun. Shifting patterns play on the platform and the ground below as the sun arcs across the sky. Steel pipes form a dignified, vernacular order of columns under the trellis, small sections nesting like capitals at the top. The columns were inspired by historic structures in the Denver area, expressing western values of pragmatism and durability.

The park retrieves memories of Denver's Native American heritage. Visitors first come to the new city street named for Little Raven, who originally welcomed white settlers to the city and maintained friendships from his big tipi. Then, near the widest part of the park, the ground rises gradually in a broad, 40-foot-high cone to its new high point, called Overlook Hill. The hill is crowned with a sunken amphitheater called Sky Garden, a destination for experiencing the dome of the heavens in the center of the city. In the quiet and simple setting of Sky Garden, cardinal directions are marked by the placement of four black granite benches. Removed from the bright light of downtown buildings, this is a popular place for solstice celebrations and star-gazing on summer nights.

A network of paved trails provides plenty of walking opportunity for residents of downtown Denver, and a generous number of benches offer places to rest and relax. From a series of gateway promontories along Little Raven Street, the trails thread through the park to a footbridge across the river.

And there are more places for meeting, climbing, and surveying the scenery. One end of the park eddies around a large egg-shaped terraced green defined by curving concrete steps. The turf-covered top and the perimeter steps offer another ideal place to view the stillness of the Denver skyline and the motion of the clouds, river, and prairie grasses.

Jones & Jones provided schematic landscape design and complete architectural services for Commons Park as a member of the design team led by Civitas of Denver.

View of the green open space with English Oaks and the 15th Street Bridge beyond.

View of the seating stairs and Bridge Plaza overlook beyond.

Aerial view of Commons Park, looking north toward Denver's downtown.

LEFT: Volleyball Court on the south meadow.

BELOW: View of cord grass and wild flowers in the river swales.

RIGHT: View across the Platte River to the Bridge Plaza and Meadow.

BELOW RIGHT: View of the meandering pedestrian path through the park's promenade.

ABOVE LEFT: Prairie uplands area with the park's comfort station structure.

FAR LEFT: View of the red sandstone comfort station with shade trellis.

LEFT: Detail of the red sandstone walls of the Bridge Plaza overlook.

ABOVE: View of cord grass gardens with Bridge Plaza trellis shade structure beyond.

RIGHT: View from Sky Garden of mixed use housing under development along the park's edge.

TOP LEFT: View of restored native vegetation below the Belvedere.

LEFT: Native wildflowers along the edge of the south meadow.

ABOVE: Kayaker shooting the rapids below Trappers Landing.

ARCTIC RING OF LIFE COMPLEX

DETROIT, MICHIGAN

2001

Nunavut, Inuit for "Our Land," is a newly named Canadian Territory around Hudson Bay, just about fifteen degrees in latitude above Detroit and extending to the Arctic Circle. With the completion of the Arctic Ring of Life exhibit and companion facilities at the Detroit Zoo, the city has made a lasting connection with Nunavut.

Detroit has also made a giant step into the future of zoos. The 4.2-acre exhibit replaces a small moated and walled-off polar bear exhibit built in 1928. The bears were crowded and alone then. Now they share their man-made tundra with arctic foxes, seals, and snowy owls. With the new exhibit and the addition of more bears for a total of seven, the Detroit Zoo has the largest polar bear collection in the nation.

Sparsely populated and as large as Alaska and California combined, Nunavut is alive with the seasons of the tundra, the icy marine world, the animals, and the culture of the people, as zoo visitors are finding out.

Nunavut has two major predators: polar bears and humans. While each species has occasionally preyed on the other, their relationship is more spiritual than survival-based. The intricacies of that relationship inspired several facets of the exhibit. Here, the bears are seen as part of a larger ecosystem and also part of the Inuit circle of life.

The landscape offers a reading of the ways of the Inuit people and how they view the bears as part of their world. There are rock sculptures in the landscape—boulders stacked to achieve distinctive and readable shapes and used as guides. At the entrance is a replica of an Inuit dwelling constructed with rustic tools and whalebones. Inuit artists were commissioned to craft several elements of the Arctic Ring of Life and adjoining gallery, including a nine-foot-high polar bear sculpture that welcomes visitors.

To represent the seasons of Nunavut and accommodate four animal species as part of the same exhibit, the area is divided roughly in two by a moated barrier concealed from the public. One half of the exhibit is shaped to simulate the landforms of the tundra and planted in a rich array of grasses and ground covers that show its summer side. The other is sculpted to mimic the snow and ice of winter, with a large, branching pool of salt water chilled to 55 degrees and dotted with floating ice.

Entry to Arctic Ring of Life exhibit, a landscape of tundra, pack ice, and open sea that interprets life in the northern expanses of Canada, Greenland, Norway, Russia, and Alaska (USA).

A meandering path for visitors circles the center of the exhibit, crossing from summer green to winter white. As it approaches the center of the Arctic Ring of Life, the path enters the Nunavut Gallery, a rounded structure partially submerged in the saltwater ice pool. The gallery displays paintings and sculptures by Inuit artists, and screens show videos of hunting and other vital skills that allow people to flourish in the Arctic. Floor-to-ceiling windows offer underwater views of seals and bears. Visitors leave through the Polar Passage, a spectacular glass tunnel submerged in a large saltwater pool from which they can see polar bears swimming inches overhead. The passage is crafted to simulate an ice cave, with ceilings of dripping icicles. It leads to the Exploration Station, which tells the story of modern expeditions to the Arctic and the challenges faced by scientists and explorers. Here, there are more views of underwater polar bear habitat and ice shelves in the pool.

The Arctic Ring of Life reaches far into the future of zoo design, building upon two overarching trends started by Jones & Jones. One is the evolution of zoo design as a multidisciplinary specialty driven by the landscape. Placing animals at the center of the design process has meant the dedication of larger areas of land, the reconstruction of complex ecosystems on site, and the reintroduction of visitors to animal species through the larger context of the partially reconstructed natural habitat. Many species of animals and plants typically occupy the same exhibit. Animals roam freely within larger confines, choosing to approach visitor areas or stay in remote corners.

The second trend is the concept of adding human settlement and native cultures to the mix, expressing and interpreting the ways human and natural worlds coexist and adapt to each other.

At the Arctic Ring of Life, the two go hand in hand with institutional trends at the Detroit Zoo. Animal comfort and health is a greater priority than ever before. In addition to their vastly expanded habitat, polar bears in Detroit will be able to take advantage of buried cooling pads and 300-pound blocks of ice. They will search for and find food in special caches buried in the ground.

Zoos are adopting far-reaching missions in response to global threats to certain species, such as the polar bear. The Detroit Zoo plans to take orphan cubs in the future and develop a captive breeding program. There are holding areas on site for foxes and owls, seals, and bears, respectively. Facilities for medical care, research, and breeding programs for bears, as well as offices for the curator of mammals, are co-located with the polar bear building.

At the same time, the exhibit achieves two important requirements. In addition to visitors being immersed in the habitat in ways that are exciting as well as safe, predator and prey must be visually proximate but physically separate. In the tundra part of the exhibit the bears and their natural prey—the foxes and snowy owls—are separated by two concentric barriers. Bears are circumscribed by a dry moat that is invisible from the visitor path. The foxes and owls exhibit occupy a ring between the moat and the path, constrained on the outside by invisible netting. Seals are confined to the edge of the winter habitat and occupy their own salt water pool, separated from the polar bears by transparent barriers.

The new exhibit has boosted the zoo's 1.2-million annual attendance by 15 percent. The Arctic Ring of Life also puts Detroit on the global science map, where it has become a center for animal welfare, research, and environmental education.

Jones & Jones is the architect and landscape architect of the Arctic Ring of Life Complex at the Detroit Zoo for the Detroit Zoological Institute.

BELOW: Whale Bone Structure and Inookshook markers depict the Inuit use of stone cairns or "inukshuks" as directional aids and their use of whale bone structures as summer camp shelters.

Whale Bone structure overlook, tundra exhibit area, summer scene.

Whale Bone structure overlook, tundra exhibit area, winter scene with Inookshook marker.

ABOVE: Nunavut Village. The exhibit carefully displays the landscapes and the lifeway of the Inuit.

FAR LEFT AND LEFT: The Exploration Station provides a "window" to the ice pack and water passages of the Arctic, visitors often treated to full "press" of human hand to bear claw.

BELOW: The Nunavut Gallery marks the entrance to a permanent exhibit of contemporary Inuit art and to the rarely viewed underwater world of the polar bears and seals.

ABOVE: *Inside the 70-foot-long Polar Passage, visitors experience face-to-face encounters with polar bears and seals.*

RIGHT: *A tile mural in the entry to the Nunavut Gallery depicts an artist's view of the Arctic's ring of life.*

TOP LEFT: A winter scene on the ice pack. Polar bears explore and roam along leads and polynyas (open water channels), encouraging natural "hunting" behavior.

BOTTOM LEFT: Polar Passage, an unparalleled view of the undersea world of the polar bear and the seal.

ABOVE: The Exploration Station marks the entrance of a relative newcomer to the Arctic landscape—the explorer.

RIGHT: Exploration Station exhibits explain the lure of the wild and uninhabited North and the mark of explorers on the face of the Arctic.

DUWAMISH RIVER REVIVAL PROJECTS
SEATTLE, WASHINGTON
1993-PRESENT

Seattle has a river. Hemmed in by concrete, straightened and almost invisible, it is nevertheless still very alive. Pieces of shoreline are green and inviting, thanks to neighborhood activists, interventions such as the Gateway Parks, and strategic efforts like the 2001 plan, "Duwamish Riverfront Revival: A Waterfront for Salmon and People in South Park." All of these provide a framework for bringing natural, living systems back into balance with the built environment. They present a practical model for stewarding other urbanized waterways in the 21st Century.

The city's history is tied to shipping, and its urban development is connected to the waters of its bay and lakes. The Duwamish, which feeds into the base of Elliott Bay just southwest of downtown Seattle, was once a vast, living delta marsh, rising and falling with the tides, feeding several species of salmon as they made their way from river to sea—and then back again upstream to spawn.

But the river was reshaped to fit the city's early economic ambitions. The riverine delta and estuarine habitat were all but destroyed. Salmon and the complex river system that supported them have been on the decline for over a century, the river hardened and nearly hidden within a dense cluster of heavy industry.

In the first years of the 20th Century, the city regraded a number of inconvenient hills, deliberately sluicing soils into the distributaries to the delta to claim over 800 acres of buildable land. The volume of the river flow was greatly reduced when the construction of the Lake Washington ship canal, ending in 1917, lowered the lake and diverted river tributaries like the Black River. Then the remaining channel was dredged and filled into a navigable waterway with turning basins. All the while, smaller tributaries were beheaded, piped through culverts, and filled over.

A natural Puget Sound delta distributary.

As the port developed, the natural oxbows and shallows of the channel were straightened and deepened to accommodate shipping and cargo-handling facilities. The stretches of shoreline that were not built up with mills and warehouses were paved with asphalt or concrete that remains to this day. Ninety-eight percent of the natural intertidal salmon habitat was lost.

By the end of the century, Seattle—the city made famous for its telescoped views of mountains, islands and water—had all but lost its way to the huge stream in its midst. But in the meantime, dawning environmental awareness turned local and national attention to the impacts of development on the health of the natural systems all around us. The Chinook salmon that run in the Duwamish were listed under the Endangered Species Act, increasing pressure on local governments to clean up city sewage and industrial contaminants. A string of communities along the river took up the cause, inspired by activist resident John Beal.

Now, Seattle is being reintroduced to its river. Two significant spots of green, the Gateway Parks, now bloom where street ends meet the stream bed on either side of the Duwamish.

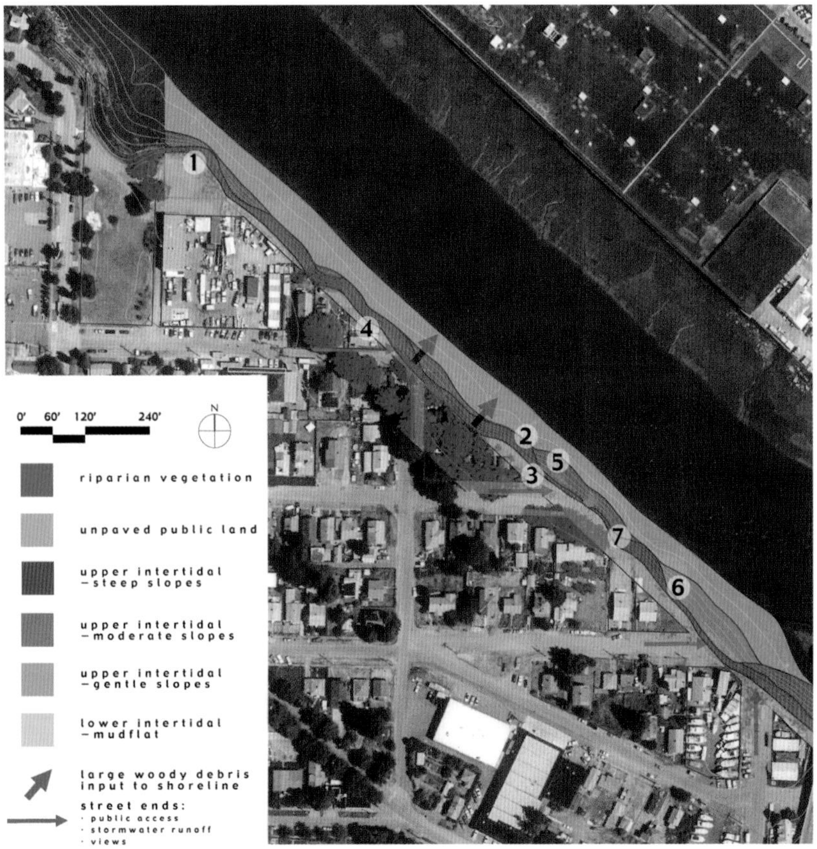

Duwamish River Project area.

On the north side, a high, grassy knoll provides an outlook within the cluttered industrial landscape south of the city. Pieces of rock and rubble with interesting shapes and bench-making qualities are recycled as seating and viewing promontories. An existing gentle ramp on one side of the park has been recast as a kayak landing. Windrows of trees are named after tributaries to the Duwamish, some of which no longer exist due to industrial development.

Through this project and the public access it has created, the whole watershed is reconnected in spirit. The work began with weeks of clearing and cleaning of the site by volunteers from surrounding neighborhoods. On Earth Day 1993, several hundred adults and schoolchildren gathered to plant 400 shrubs and 100 trees, including Wild Crabapple, Western Red Cedar, Oceanspray, Indian Plum, Flowering Currant, and Nootka Rose. Members of the Duwamish Tribe spoke to volunteers. A commemorative rock ledge was added in 2003.

On the south side of the river, another swath of green is maintained by the South Park neighborhood, helping to frame the Duwamish and set new terms for the relationship of city and river. Extending the benefit of a corporate-sponsored public access open space across the street end, this modest piece of shoreline offers a place to lean back on the grassy slope with an intimate view of the river.

Although on the surface the value of the Gateway Parks projects is largely symbolic, they serve as a powerful focus for community interest and energy, energy that continues to bring resources to the river and its salmonid habitat. Along with neighborhood pride, open space and public access is helping to build a network of environmental stewardship. A 2001 plan, "Duwamish Riverfront Revival: A Waterfront for Salmon and People in South Park," provides a road map for further progress. Created for a network of neighborhood and activist groups, the project is based on the knowledge that where government ownership is not possible, collaboration is essential. It provides a framework for the use of disparate but valuable resources, from the contributions of industry and local government agencies to the electricity from a boat builder next door, a speaker from the Duwamish Indian Tribe, or hundreds of yards of fill dirt from the state Department of Transportation.

By mapping the river and its shoreline habitat in terms of natural systems and real conditions, the Duwamish Riverfront Revival has brought the river out of the background of industrial development and into the light of present-day reality. The plan is a handbook for stewardship of the Duwamish, emphasizing the links between project, place, and natural systems. The goal is not to restore the natural state of the river, but to enhance selected attributes so that the river can be revived and enjoyed.

The project provides basic education in salmon life cycle and corresponding needs in the estuary environment, as well as a primer on habitat structure and biotechnical enhancement. There is graphic and historic exploration of the neighborhood along the Duwamish and its opportunities for greater connection to the river. The document provides tools for evaluating potential projects for success and cost effectiveness. It also outlines funding strategies and identifies sources of support, including government agencies seeking habitat restoration to settle natural resource damage claims. There are permitting strategies for projects designed around habitat restoration and salmon recovery. Finally, the plan tells the story of successful grassroots efforts at restoration and river access.

The Gateway Parks are proving that a modest park project can become the center of a movement. It's a movement that has been joined by University of Washington and University of Oregon architecture and landscape architecture students, through the Jones & Jones Field School, starting in the summer of 2003. By encouraging students to "weave themselves into the fabric of the communities" on either side of the river and design new infrastructure for linking them together, the leaders of the Field School are helping to extend the Gateway Parks into the surrounding neighborhoods and into the future.

The Duwamish Riverfront Revival effort has harnessed environmental activism and community conscience, and that has fed the imagination of a city and a region.

Jones & Jones was master planner for the Duwamish Riverfront Revival for the Environmental Coalition of South Seattle. Jones & Jones provided pro bono landscape architecture services and field coordination for the grassroots effort to build Gateway Parks.

The delta is squared off at Harbor Island.

Duwamish before.

Earth Day sign-in.

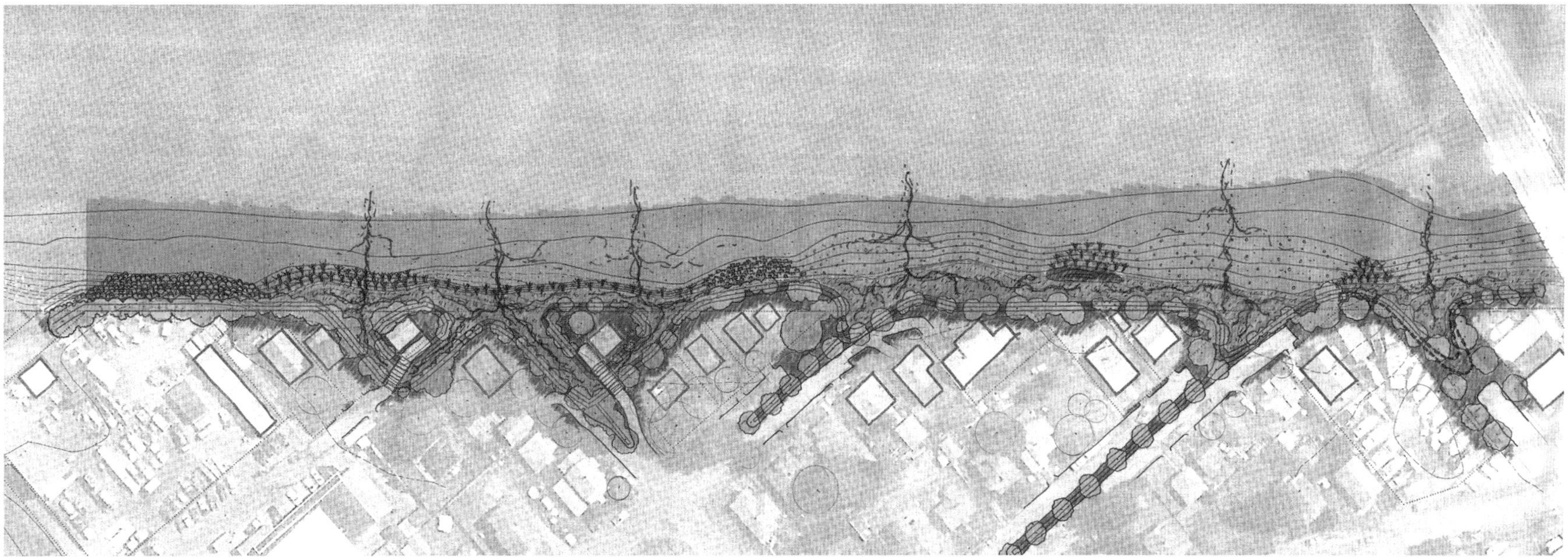

Duwamish River Revival.

LEFT: Mt. Rainier looms to the south.

BELOW: Slip Four Park.

RIGHT: Knolls in the containers.

BELOW RIGHT: Industrial activity on the river.

TOP LEFT: Knoll on the South Park side.

LEFT: Knoll on the Georgetown side.

ABOVE: Accessing the river.

ICICLE CREEK MUSIC CENTER
LEAVENWORTH, WASHINGTON
2001

Peaceful, contemplative, resonant with nature, Icicle Creek Music Center is a mountain setting for music education and performance. But like the music and the rugged landscape, the architecture is challenging. Using traditional construction techniques, the buildings are essentially modern, and form follows function with rigorous discipline and economy. The chiseled angles of the buildings reflect the rocky escarpment and pine forest of Icicle Canyon. At the same time, the interiors yield excellent acoustics.

A 120-person recital hall, six free-standing practice buildings and an open meadow stage and amphitheater are set along the river at the toe of a weathered granite knoll. Lodges and support facilities for 40 are clustered nearby. The center offers residence programs for chamber groups, youth symphonies, and visiting musicians from jazz to bluegrass. The campus also provides a base for music educators, institute retreats and seminars, and a stage for local and regional events and performances throughout the year.

Icicle Creek Music Center grew along with planning for an adjacent project, Sleeping Lady Mountain Retreat. They were both developed by Icicle Creek founder Harriett Bullitt. The sister projects share a number of facilities at Sleeping Lady, including a dining hall, conference rooms, and library facilities, all interconnected with footpaths.

At the heart of the Icicle Creek campus is the wedge-shaped Canyon Wren Recital Hall. At the wide end, a multi-paned glass wall presents a sweeping mountain view, framing Sleeping Lady herself—the profile of a reclining woman in the distant ridgeline. Like all of the music facilities at Icicle Creek, the recital hall is open in plan and adaptable to many different seating arrangements for rehearsal, performance, and recording. Even for concerts, there is no formal separation between players and audience. Musical groups can play facing the windows and the mountains, or they can turn to face the audience with the view—filtered by an abstract pattern of colored glass panes—as a backdrop. In any configuration, rich sound and scenery envelop everyone inside.

The walls of the recital hall act in concert to bring excellent acoustics to diverse performances. The tall and wide window wall reflects sound, and the short wall on the opposite side is canted forward and textured to capture it. One of the long interior walls of the recital hall is a func-

ABOVE: View to main entry of Canyon Wren Recital Hall. ABOVE RIGHT: View of musicians' practice unit set in a meadow of native grasses.

tional work of art: articulated maple panels are placed within a horizontal frame to form a complex composition, acting as a giant sound diffuser. The long wall opposite plays a more passive role in the acoustics of the hall, with a flush panel. The functional walls are punctuated by exposed steel and laminated wood diagonals, which brace the roof structure for snow loads. The grand recital hall space is supported by a greenroom, storage area, and other support facilities in the building.

A series of six individual and group practice buildings stand along the base of the granite knoll that dominates the site. Immersed in the natural landscape, the complex geometries of the diminutive practice rooms make them highly tuned, personal sound chambers that underscore the importance of individual commitment to art. Two larger practice rooms for ensembles are equipped with grand pianos. A large window in each, softened by recycled colored glass panels, brings nature into the session.

Following the legacy of Sleeping Lady Mountain Retreat, Icicle Creek is designed to push standards of sustainable development. Stormwater from the roof of the recital hall passes through a bioswale into a seasonal pond, minimizing runoff into the river. Geothermal source heat pumps provide heat to the recital hall in winter and cooling in summer. Mature trees, saved throughout the site, provide protection from seasonal and daily temperature fluctuations. Sleeping lodges, which are equipped with kitchens to accommodate small groups, cluster around a large granite boulder under mature trees.

Buildings were designed to accommodate standard construction materials and techniques. Local contractors were involved in all phases of the project, working with the design team and adapting conventional materials and methods to sustainable objectives and new technologies. Greater wall stud spacing and a composite structure of steel frame with laminated wood beams minimizes the depth of large-span structural timbers and the total quantity of framing lumber. Benches, door stock, and interior trim came from forest windfall reclamation and from local demolition projects.

From chamber music to bluegrass and jazz, Icicle Creek Music Center hosts regional events and musical performances in the recital hall throughout the year. On summer evenings, an audience of up to 400 gathers in a meadow amphitheater to watch performances on an open air stage. Icicle Creek Music Center is becoming a base for a music community that reaches far beyond the Icicle Valley.

Jones & Jones was architect and landscape architect for the Icicle Creek Music Center for Harriet Bullitt, owner.

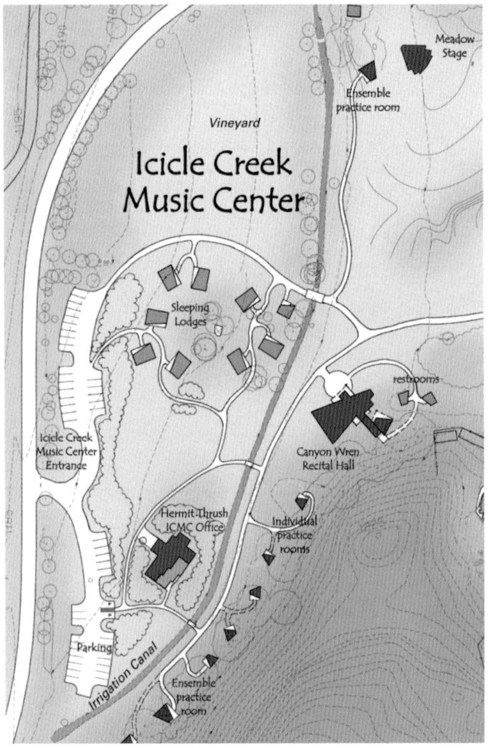

Icicle Creek Music Center campus plan.

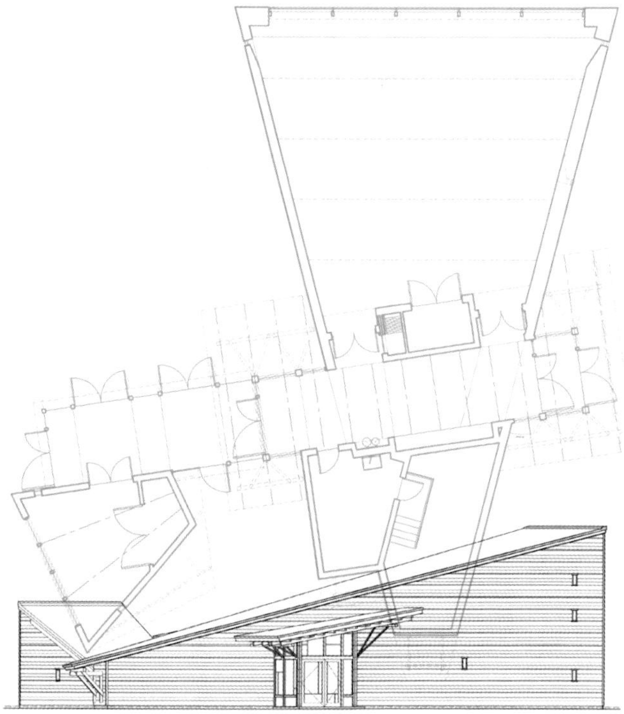

Architectural drawings of the Recital Hall plan and elevation.

TOP LEFT: The north wall of the Canyon Wren Recital Hall is built with articulated maple panels that diffuse and condition the sound within the space.

TOP RIGHT: Canyon Wren Recital Hall view window has a patterned curtain wall system and colored glass that breaks the large view window into smaller scaled vignettes. Solar shade is drawn to reduce summer solar gain.

ABOVE: Main entry to the Canyon Wren Recital Hall. The angled building form reflects the surrounding granite mountains.

LEFT: Musicians' sleeping lodges with the canyon wall beyond. Mountain vernacular architectural materials in a simple, modern form.

BELOW: Musicians' sleeping lodges grouped around a cluster of second-growth fir trees and a large granite boulder. Each sleeping unit's large window focuses on trees, mountains, or granite rocks.

RIGHT: Generous entry canopy on the left continues through the building, serving as the lobby space, and continues to the enclosed walkway between the musicians' greenroom and the Recital Hall. Icicle Canyon's Sleeping Lady ridge formation is in the distance.

BELOW RIGHT: Small practice units reflect the Recital Hall shape and form and cluster along the toe of the north-facing granite knoll with views into trees, meadows, and rock boulder slopes, connecting each musician with the natural environment.

NATIONAL MUSEUM OF THE AMERICAN INDIAN
WASHINGTON, D.C.
2004

With flowing lines and earth-based architecture, the National Museum of the American Indian and its landscape are profoundly disorienting. This is as it should be.

The context sets the stage. The building claims a prominent site on the National Mall directly in front of the U.S. Capitol, surrounded by neoclassicist structures. As the latest addition to the Smithsonian Institution, the new museum invokes and reflects a heritage that has been largely denied or overlooked since the institution was founded. The 420,000-square-foot building is home to one of the most complete rotating collections of Native American art and artifacts in the world, showcasing history from the pre-contact era to the present day.

While the envelope of the structure fits inside the basic restrictions of its site in the National Mall group, the character of the museum contrasts markedly with its neighbors. It is a celebration of the spirit of nature as well as the memories and living cultures of Native peoples.

Based on years of dialog with Native Americans in their own communities, the National Museum of the American Indian is the product of many fathers and mothers. It is conceived as a tribal elder in stone and mortar, intended to teach generations of Americans about their Native American heritage. Its inviting, organic forms and open spaces welcome millions every year.

As if carved by wind or water on its 4.25-acre trapezoidal site, the swirling, braiding lines of the five-story structure defy simple geometries. Like the edge of a massive stone cliff face, undulating walls form shelves and overhangs. Extending upward from the base, the Kasota limestone changes textures from coarse to very smooth, giving the whole building a presence both flowing and grounded.

The interior plan is dominated by circular spaces. Circles are a recurring theme in storytelling, governance, and building in many traditional Native American cultures. Think of the kiva or the tipi. At the museum, gathering spaces flow together in rounded rooms on the first level. As visitors make their way to the stairways and the collections on the upper levels, the swirling lines of paving flow and braid together along with the curving walls. Although the main rooms are distinct—each with a center and a purpose—there are no hard lines to mark the thresholds or endings.

Within the fluid sculpture of the building itself, a core set of traditional Native American cultural references guided myriad decisions about spatial arrangement, expressive details, and art. These elements reorient the building and its visitors to the natural world and the meanings it has held for Native Americans.

TOP: A view of the museum's east elevation with a 50-foot overhang at the main entry that provides shelter to arriving visitors. The wetland landscape in the foreground reflects the organic building forms, while providing a habitat for local animal communities.

ABOVE: The building's south side landscape area is planted with domesticated plant crops of the American Indians, including corn, tobacco, and potatoes.

The four cardinal directions determine axes in plan and placement of interior openings and fenestration. The seasonal path of the sun, moon, and stars is celebrated through various architectural and artistic devices. The river, an important element in the lives and cultures of Native Americans everywhere, is present as well. The National Mall is located near the Potomac River, and the heart of the museum is a large, round hall and gathering place—its name, "Potomac," recapitulates the original Piscataway word, which means "where the goods are brought in." In addition to the openings, the natural light, and the astronomical references, large artworks and changing wall textures provide orientation inside the building.

The entry plaza faces the east to greet the morning sun, and the paving pattern records lunar events. In this space, visitors can take shelter beneath one of the overhangs formed by the upper levels of the museum building, shelves inspired by the carved rock cliffs of the Americas. Just inside the main doors, hundreds of Native American words meaning "welcome" are projected onto a screen in a continually changing wall. The doors into the Potomac are etched with sun symbols from Native cultures.

The Potomac is topped by a dome 120 feet in diameter, soaring to 120 feet. At the top, an oculus admits sunlight throughout the day. Inlaid at the center of the floor is a disk of red stone, to symbolizing the heart or center of the space. From this circle a clear view extends in four cardinal directions to the outside. The space is alive with the motion of the heavens: solstices are mapped on the axes with rings of red and black granite in the floor. Openings in the southern side of the main floor hold eight acrylic prisms crafted by artist Charles Ross. Activated by the angle of the sun at the solstice and equinox they send rainbows into the spaces inside. Evoking Native basketry and textiles, a wall of woven copper bands encircles the ceremonial space of the Potomac.

The museum holds several circular theaters of varying sizes. The main, 320-seat theater is designed for storytelling, with superb acoustics, multi-media projection systems, and language translation systems. Vertical paneling evokes a hardwood forest, and the dark ceiling twinkles with constellations. The 120-seat Lelawl Theater is specially designed for a multimedia introduction to the museum exhibits. Just outside the Potomac, a 140-seat amphitheater is ready for dance performances and special celebrations.

A Mitsitsam café adjoining the Potomac is designed to express the cultural connection between Native Americans and the gathering and sharing of food, and menus are based on an array of traditional foodstuffs and recipes. Café and museum landscape, which includes stands of native corn species on the south side, emphasize Native American agricultural traditions.

A grand stairway, marked by a specially commissioned totem pole, is the portal from the Potomac into the exhibit spaces. The lighted cases of an upscale museum shop glow from the base. Near the top of the stairway, another shop is wrapped with curved, hand-adzed cedar boards for a sweep of warm, earthy color and rich texture. The cedar wall is just one example of many intensely crafted elements in the museum.

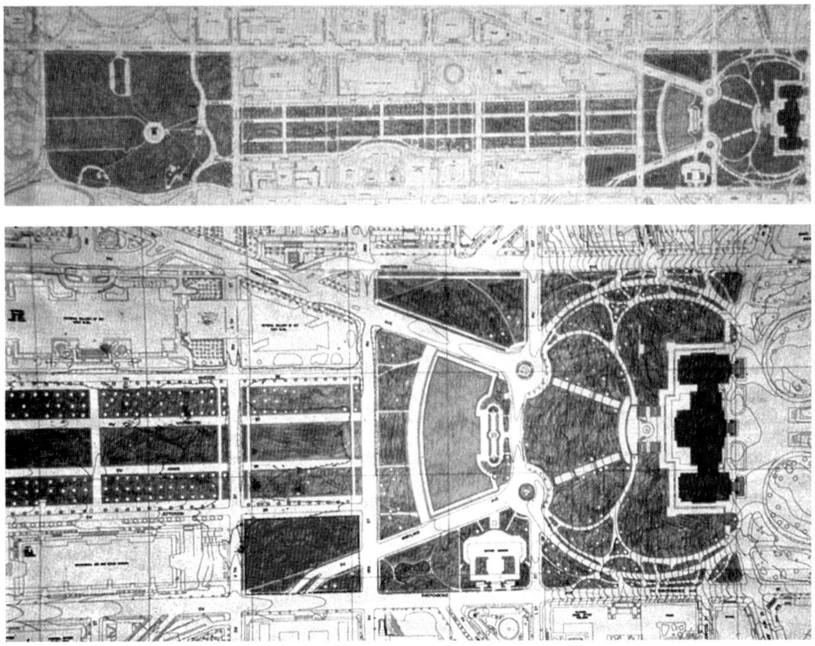

The NMAI site (shown in red) is located at the east end of the National Mall.

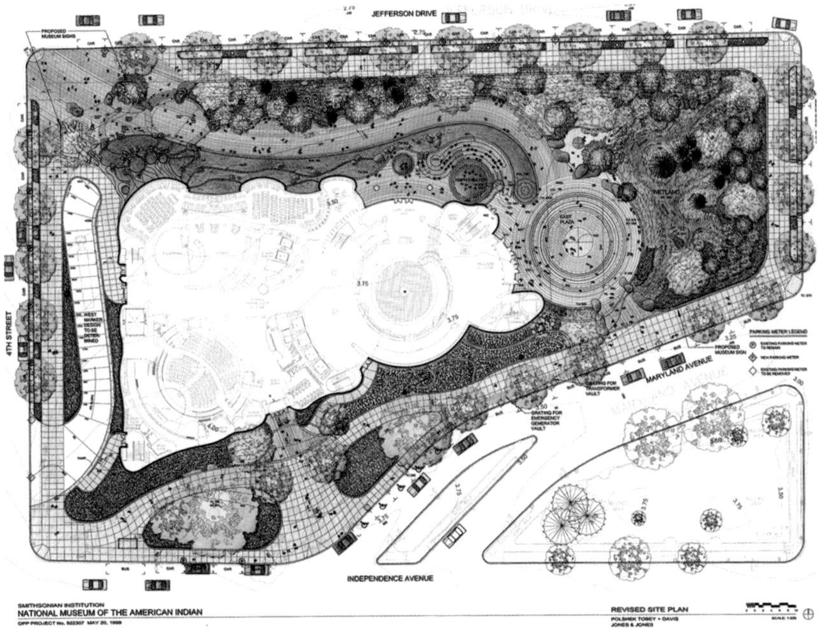

Site plan showing the East Welcome Plaza, wetland area, surround naturalized landscape, and hardscape design.

The landscape and water feature just outside the building walls are rich in content and opportunities for interaction. The landscape presents several distinct environments in the Eastern lowlands of the continent. More than 33,000 plants of 150 species are gathered in habitats that represent woodlands, wetlands, meadows, and traditional croplands.

Twenty-four large rocks and boulders, known as "grandfather rocks," give the landscape its own character and spatial references and serve as elders greeting museum visitors as they approach the building. Naturally hewn by the winds and rains of millions of years and weighing up to 30 tons, they were selected by the design team, sent by the Montagnass First Nation group in Mashteulatsh, Quebec, and received with ceremonies of blessing. Special stones representing the four Cardinal Directions mark the north-south and east-west axes of the museum grounds, axes that intersect in the Potomac area of the museum interior. These markers are directly linked to sacred places and living tribal communities all over the Americas, coming from the banks of Acasta Lake in the Northwest Territories (Dogrib); Isla Navarino in Southern Chile (Yagan); Keamoku Lava Flow in Hilo, Hawaii (Kapuna); and Monocacy Valley, Maryland (several mid-Atlantic tribes, including the Piscataway-Conoy, Accohanack, Assateague, and Monocan).

A large water feature dominates the north side of the building, cooling the site on hot summer days and welcoming visitors to the Mall. At grade, the primary material changes from golden limestone to deep gray American-mist granite in the pools and runnels. Evoking Tiber Creek, which once flowed through the site, the water begins as a powerful cascade tumbling over boulders and ends as a peaceful pool near the museum entrance.

A discrete offering area, surrounded by boulders, provides a place for reflection and contemplation and an opportunity to leave special items of offering. An outdoor theater is located on the north side of the museum, adjacent to the Potomac. When doors are open at event times, visitors and performers can move directly in and out of the building.

With its many authors and its expression of natural, dynamic forces, the museum is conceived as a living thing. Although most visitors won't notice as they wait at the entry, the stone pavement of the plaza maps the night sky over Washington on November 28, 1989. It's a birthday, the date of the legislation establishing the National Museum of the American Indian.

As part of a complex design team assembled by the Smithsonian Institution for the National Museum of the American Indian, Jones & Jones provided architecture (along with SmithGroup in association with Lou Weller, the Native American Design Collaborative, and Polshek Partnership Architects) and landscape architecture (along with Donna House and EDAW). Project designers were Douglas Cardinal Ltd. and GBQC, Johnpaul Jones, Ramona Sakiestewa, and Donna House.

Study model for the 4,000-square-foot Ronaok Market Place gift shop located on the 2nd floor.

Study model of the west side of the Potomac space interior, with basket-like stepped dome and oculus.

TOP LEFT: Made of American mist granite, the "Welcoming Plaza" outside the museum's main entry provides for gatherings and celebrations during various times of the year.

TOP: Detail view of the unique copper screen that defines the circular public gathering space known as the Potomac.

ABOVE: The building exterior is clad in "Kasota" limestone, a rich, yellow and ochre colored stone from Minnesota. The building's base is made with unfinished rough back blocks; the main body of the building is made with blocks of split face stone.

LEFT: An integrated waterfall cascade welcomes the visitor with sound, reflective natural light, and fresh cooling air. The waterfall stone is made with layers carefully integrated into the building form.

ABOVE: The main entry on the east side of the museum is sheltered from summer to winter weather with its large overhanging roof forms.

ABOVE RIGHT: Large boulders known as "grandfather rocks" are located around the main entry path and welcome arriving visitors.

RIGHT: The east entry overhang is supported by a column with a three-stepped stone architectural form.

ABOVE: The floor of the Potomac viewed from above shows the circular "heart" of the building. The small center circle of red stone represents fire, traditionally marking the center of Native American gathering spaces. The wood floor is for dance demonstrations and other American Indian activities.

RIGHT: The interior Potomac space was designed for American Indian performances, where visitors at all levels can hear and see the beauty of the "living museum."

LEFT: Interior view of the museum's main public entry; the stone and plaster walls and copper screen reinforce the organic flow of the spaces and building materials.

ABOVE: The NMAI galleries tell stories of contemporary American Indian people using their art and their craft. This gallery's theme is Native Modernism.

PARIS-LEXINGTON ROAD RECONSTRUCTION
PARIS TO LEXINGTON, KENTUCKY
2002

On the long curves of the Paris-Lexington Road in Kentucky, motorists get much more than another trip. They get to experience the contours and character of the land, as fresh as the new-mown grass and as old as time.

The 12-mile length of reconstructed highway offers a clear vision of the future of road design. That's because it's landscape-driven: traffic algorithms follow. Driver safety and ease go hand in hand with community health and scenic quality.

Commonly called "the old limestone highway" or Paris Pike, the highway runs through the heart of the Bluegrass Region, connecting Lexington, a center of economic growth, and Paris, a much smaller city surrounded by farming and mounting development. Paris Pike is wholly contained in a 10,000-acre historic district eligible for listing on the National Register of Historic Places. This district contains several individual properties already listed.

Paris Pike is a popular part of any tour of the Bluegrass Region. Residual savanna, woodlands, and hedgerows frame the open pastures and fields along the corridor. The fertile, rolling landscape is an ideal setting for horse farms and contains one of the largest concentrations of prizewinning thoroughbred farms and breeding operations in the world. The Pike is lined with 200-year-old rock fences, and it passes by ancient trees and antebellum mansions with formal gated entrances, huge barns, and many other symbols of the area's horse racing and agricultural traditions.

Although it is a U.S. Highway, the old Pike had two lanes, no shoulders, insufficient right and left turn lanes, and poor sight distances. Historically, the fatality rate was more than twice that of comparable routes. Beginning in 1966, plans for turning the Pike into a four-lane highway were locked up in a hard-fought tug-of-war between those who would rebuild and widen the highway and those who advocated preservation of the historic landscape and roadway. A road-widening project approved in 1973 was stopped because of fears about impacts upon historic places.

Then a series of fatal crashes in the mid-1980s brought the proposed project back into the fore. Finally, after nearly another decade, the final

The reconstructed highway is designed to move around important resources, including ancient trees.

design team made up of engineers, landscape architects, and historians was selected and the deadlock broken. In a significant departure from tradition, landscape architects were granted considerable authority over the roadway alignment, with engineers refining the layout in the final stages of design.

The landscape architects traced the history, character, and resources of the corridor, fence by fence and farm by farm. They examined historic paths and ancient trees, walked pastures, and talked to long-time landowners along the way. In the process, they identified six landscape districts along the route.

The six districts encompass eighteen separate "rooms" distinguished by topology, vegetation, viewsheds, and cultural features. Each one is named for a side road crossing, geographic marker, or other prominent landmark. The use of place names, such as Houston Creek and Muir Station, helped to earn the trust of the local community and property owners. Increasing support for the design grew through incremental participation.

The redesign of the road is based on continuous curvilinear alignment. Established design guidelines were successfully used to curve and bend the new highway so that it fits gracefully into the rolling, pastoral landscape. Long curves are linked so that there are few sections of straight roadway.

In the new alignment, a split roadway interweaves with the old route, with southbound and northbound lanes alternately following close to the old road alignment. In this way, new capacity and safety is built into the Paris Pike while the intimate connection with the historic landscape is maintained.

Throughout the 12-mile corridor, features of the terrain are preserved within the median. Low cuts and fills are graded and create a seamless transition between highway and adjacent terrain. By designing two roadways to move independently—vertically as well as horizontally—the highway blends with the rolling landscape.

The verdant pastures and lawns of adjoining farms and estates come right up to the highway pavement. Unlike typical highways, Paris Pike has a reinforced grass shoulder instead of a paved one. Grass shoulders reduce the perceived width of the pavement and the overall visual impact of the highway. Roadway appurtenances were modified for Paris Pike. Steel-backed timber guardrails are compatible with the wood fences in the landscape. Concrete barriers and bridge abutments are clad in native limestone to match the stone walls and buildings along the corridor.

The multi-stage construction project has yielded more ties to the past. Excavations revealed early properties owned by freed slaves, bringing a "new" historic resource to the attention of the public. Conservationists discovered and saved patches of Running Buffalo Clover, an endangered plant species that was largely eradicated with the spread of pastures. Native cane was reintroduced into a creek along the reconstructed road.

Among the most distinctive features of the Paris Pike scenery are the miles of stone fences that mark property lines or follow streams and creeks; most of them remain undisturbed in their historic setting. But in reconstructing Paris Pike, three miles of stone fence were altered and rebuilt—the largest stone fence construction project in Kentucky. A master stonemason from Scotland was brought to Lexington to conduct three separate training courses and create a certification program. As a result, there is a new generation of masons capable of replacing stone fences where they once had to be removed or allowed to deteriorate.

The new Paris Pike has become a model for road reconstruction, bringing past and future together in communities once threatened by a construction project. Blended with the landscape, the new road has restored poetic beauty to an important part of the Bluegrass country.

Jones & Jones was landscape architect for the Paris-Lexington Road Reconstruction for the Kentucky Transportation Cabinet, with H.W. Lochner, engineer and primary consultant. Landscape architecture services included corridor selection and roadway alignment design.

The "Opportunity Zone" for additional two lanes of highway is superimposed on an aerial photo.

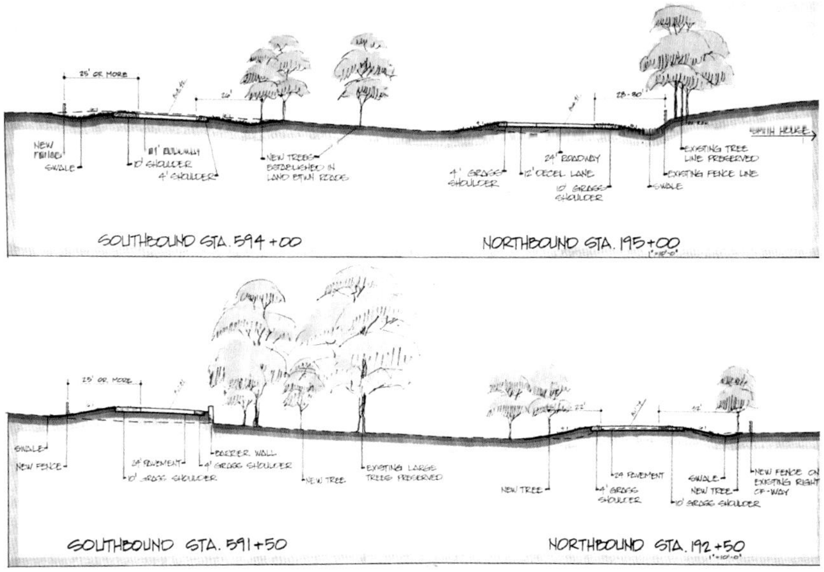

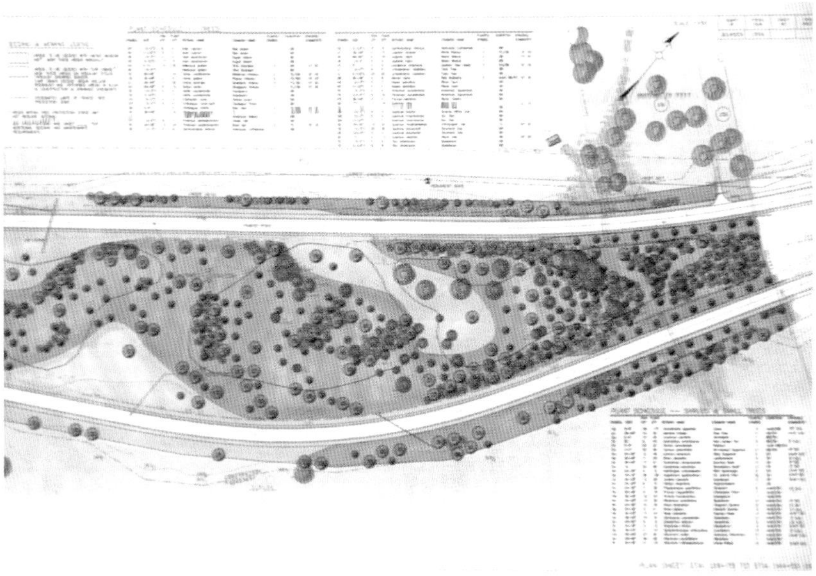

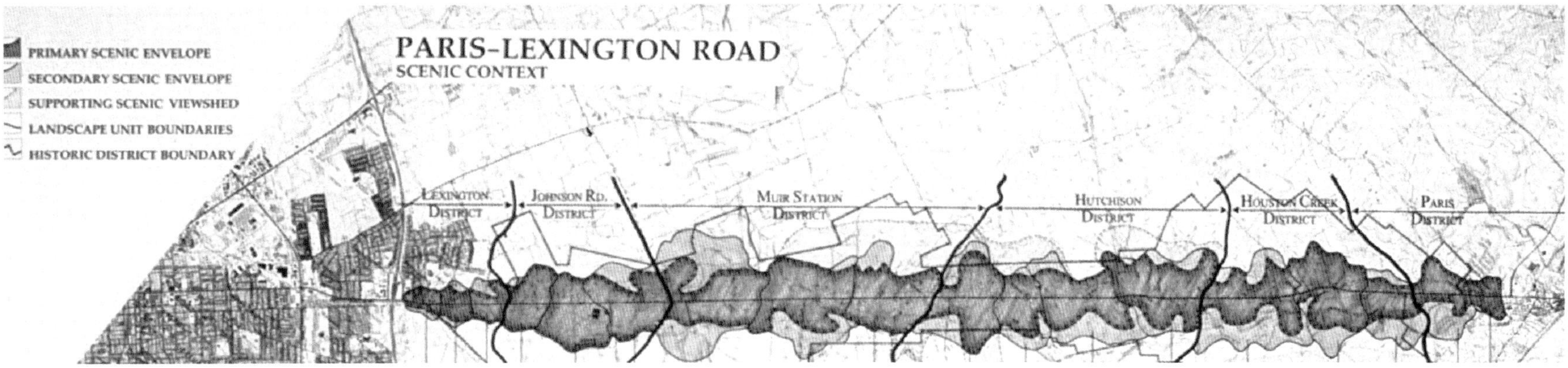

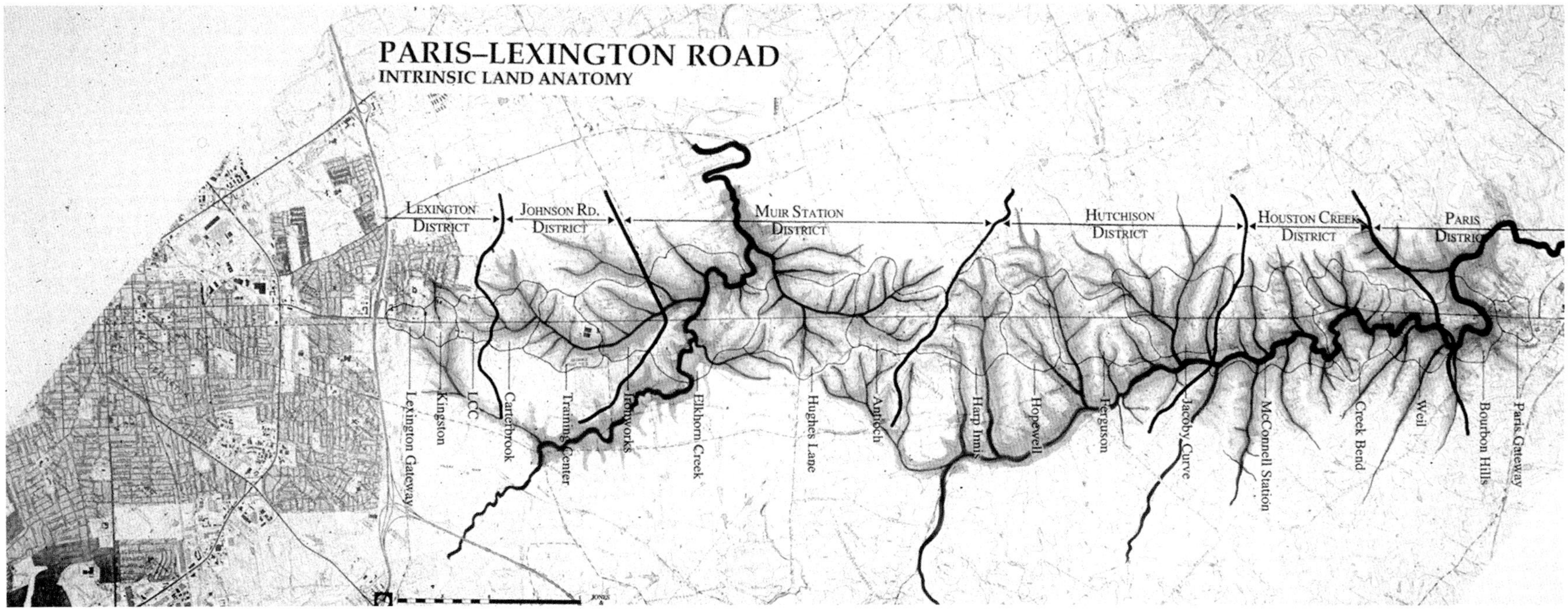

TOP LEFT: Tree Sections; TOP RIGHT: Colored plan; CENTER: Scenic Context Plan; ABOVE: Paris Pike Land Anatomy.

LEFT: The reconstructed highway weaves through a remnant of the savanna that once covered much of the Inner Bluegrass.

BELOW: Two-hundred-year-old stone fences, which are a fundamental feature of the Paris Pike landscape, were preserved to the greatest extent possible. Fences were rebuilt across farm fields wherever they were disturbed or removed.

RIGHT: All elements of the reconstructed highway were given careful consideration. This new bridge over North Elkhorn Creek is designed to be consistent with adjacent buildings and the gateways and walls at Elmendorf and Gainesway Farms.

BELOW RIGHT: Highway retaining walls and culvert headwalls are clad with native stone to blend with historic stone fences and buildings.

RIO NUEVO MASTER PLAN
TUCSON, ARIZONA
2002

The rapid development of Tucson threatens its historic identity and its present-day livability. This is a predicament it shares with many American cities. But the city is working toward a future that is all its own, based on the city's own multicultural roots and stunning natural heritage. Rio Nuevo is its ten-year plan, designed to turn sprawling Tucson around and give it a lively center.

It is a flexible vision based on a bold, unifying idea: natural systems that have been disrupted and damaged by development can be coaxed back from the edges into the heart of the city—and celebrated in the streets and public squares. Most important, Rio Nuevo shows that a plan centered upon natural systems and public green spaces is one that can bring a divided citizenry together.

Unlike the pace of recent development, Rio Nuevo can't be hurried. More than a plan redevelopment, it's a healing strategy for a city that has been torn and frayed. First a freeway sliced down the middle, separating the west side—with its old riverbed and historic settlements—from the commercial center and the traditional squares on the east side. Then, blocks of impoverished but well-established Hispanic neighborhoods along the eastern edge of the freeway were cleared for construction of a convention center.

Memories of displaced neighbors in the barrios are fresh, along with resentment toward the city for insensitive construction. The massive walls of the Tucson Convention Center are everyday reminders to citizens that top-down planning and isolated mega-projects are poor approaches to revitalization. With a poverty rate of more than 20 percent, downtown Tucson has been designated a federal Empowerment Zone, qualifying it for tax credits designed to attract development.

The city faces enormous challenges. Rapidly spreading, auto-dependent housing development and commercial strips mean that much of the area looks like Anywhere, USA. Single-family neighborhoods and isolated condominium clusters continue to take over the surrounding Sonoran Desert. At the same time, successful preservation efforts and arts investments have brought commitment to cultural diversity and the renewal of public life.

Rio Nuevo builds on these successes in an inclusive way, weaving ecology, history, architecture, and the arts into a vision for the future. The roots of the plan, as well as its name, lie in reclaiming the Santa Cruz River for public access and recreational use. The cultural and natural landscapes of the city come together on the riverbanks and floodplain.

Access to river terraces, sandbars, and islands provides opportunities for traditional cultural activities; reclaimed water is used to restore the river.

Along with plants and animals, generations of desert dwellers have sought life-giving water, cooling comfort, and the company of others along the banks of the stream. The water has slowed to a tiny trickle with intermittent high storm water carving deep into the earth, but traces of the river's rich ecology and generative power remain. And so does the geography of imagination and memory around the river.

A series of workshops with barrio residents uncovered these memories. Although they don't bring their own children there, residents told stories of visiting the river on holidays when they were small. While they may argue over investments in facilities for culture and economic development, they agree on the need to connect with the natural world in and around the city.

The heart of the Rio Nuevo plan is a healing landscape intimately linked with the forgotten history and archaeological sites on the east side of the divided city.

The vision begins with the restoration of the river. Reconstructed islands and sandbars slow the water down to a more even and natural pace, providing resting places for fish, birds, and other wildlife. New weirs and ponds accelerate the process of reclaiming habitat. Banks and terraces support new plantings of indigenous cottonwoods, willows, Arizona ash, and other riparian trees and shrubs.

Sentinel Peak, a cone rising out of the desert near the banks of the river and its original settlements, is a familiar landmark in Tucson. In the plan, mountain and river connect once again through a restored Cienega, or desert marsh and watering hole. The mountain itself, a mesquite shrubland and paloverde upland habitat that once served as an Indian burial ground, is restored as a functioning wilderness park with a trail network.

The re-greened and accessible Cienega is accompanied by restored Acequias, or irrigation ditches, first built by the native Hohokam farmers growing corn in the floodplain more than 1,000 years ago. Through uncovered foundations, the round dwellings of the Pima Indians are interpreted for contemporary residents and visitors. Although virtually nothing remains of the late-18th Century adobe Mission San Augustin and the Convento—which has been called the birthplace of Tucson—the site is designated as an interpretive center that presents the results of an archeological dig.

With strands of green extending throughout the plan, the restored Santa Cruz nourishes the urban landscape and its new pedestrian environment. Wildlife corridors cross the freeway and flow into the streets, parks, and plazas of Tucson. The natural and spiritual extension of the river environment supports the most basic goal of redevelopment efforts: to reconnect the east and west sides of a city divided by a north-south freeway, and to bring new cultural and economic vitality to the neglected west side.

Under the plan, major investments are directed to the construction of a cultural plaza, a new center on the west side that includes an international *mercado* as well as homes for the Arizona State Museum, the American Indian Cultural Center, the Santa Cruz River Interpretive Center, the Tucson Regional Visitor's Center, and the Arizona Historical Society. These new developments bracket the riverbed, with a pedestrian parkway on the west bank and a vehicular one on the east side of the river and the western edge of the freeway. The entire plaza complex is tied to a new civic plaza in downtown Tucson by a tree-lined boulevard and series of new freeway crossings for traffic and pedestrians. Eventually, the plan calls for depressing and lidding a section of freeway in order to reconnect the older barrios and new west side developments with the entertainment district of downtown Tucson.

Located near the convention center, the civic plaza is anchored by the Arizona Sonora Desert Museum, the Tucson Science Center, the Tucson Children's Museum, and the Sonoran Sea Museum as well as a large-format theater, hotels and retail, and new conference space. Reflecting pools and a fountain welcome residents and visitors, proclaiming the civic character of the plaza. A new streetcar line and tree plantings along the boulevard link it to established cultural and historic attractions on the existing Plaza de Armas, next to city hall and the Tucson Museum of Art.

All of these elements work to get people on their feet and out into the open air. Throughout the new network of public buildings, squares, and open spaces, the life-giving presence of the river springs up in the form of indigenous plantings and carefully placed water features.

Rio Nuevo represents hope for Tucson and for any city that is losing its connection with its past and its natural setting. It's a map of the future of Tucson, a city with a living center shared by all of its citizens and remembered by everyone who visits.

Jones & Jones was the urban designer for Rio Nuevo, with Hunter Interests, Inc., as prime consultant, for the City of Tucson.

LEFT: Cultural elements are brought back into the heart of Rio Nuevo's fabric, acknowledging the city's multi-cultural roots and heritage.

RIGHT: Nature is brought back and woven into the fabric of the district, an essential component of the redevelopment effort.

BELOW: Cultural Park, open air amphitheater.

BOTTOM: Workshop charrettes focused on the reclamation of the river, restoration of cultural landscapes, and changing zoning to allow mixed use development.

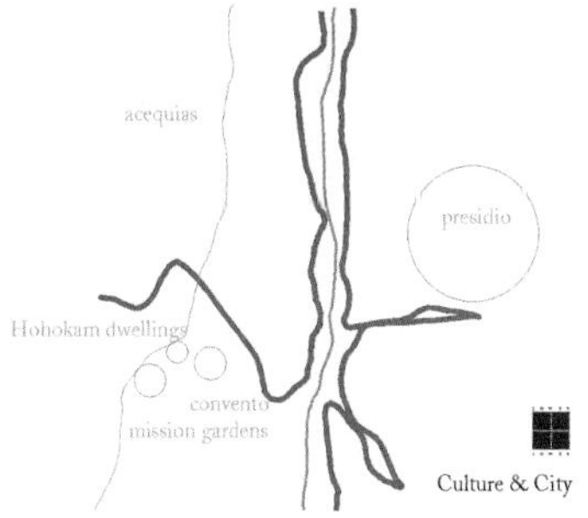

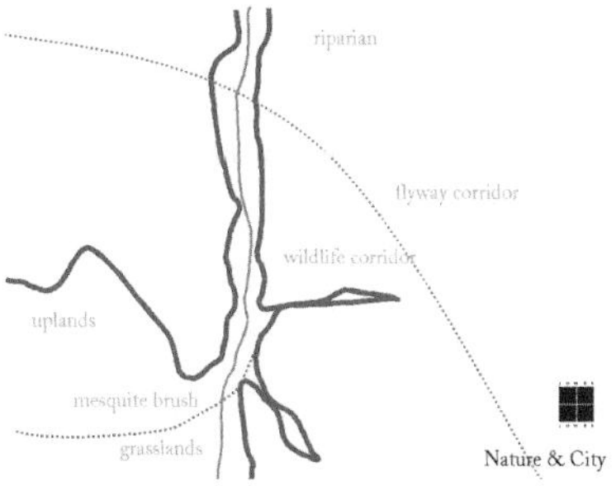

LEFT: A constructed cienega as an interpretive landscape along the nature park provides enriching educational opportunities.

BELOW AND BOTTOM: Architectural heritage—downtown near the Presidio, Westside neighborhoods and barrios.

RIGHT: View of Rio Nuevo from Sentinel Peak looking south, the Santa Cruz river at the base of the mountain.

BELOW RIGHT: Treated water brings new life to a braided river, outside of Tucson, and provides residents with a model for the restoration of the Santa Cruz river.

SLEEPING LADY MOUNTAIN RETREAT
LEAVENWORTH, WASHINGTON
1994-2003

You have to get out of your car before you arrive at Sleeping Lady Mountain Retreat, and find your way to the lobby along the trail. It's a place apart, embedded in the natural mountain environment. There could hardly be more contrast between the nearby Bavarian theme town of Leavenworth and the peaceful repose of Sleeping Lady, which takes its unique name from the profile of a mountain ridge above the retreat. The 67-acre complex lies nested around a rocky knoll near a river, sharing the site with a scattering of old-growth Ponderosa.

While visitors recharge their energies and focus their professional or personal lives, they learn how to live on the land with respect and intelligence. The footprints of the buildings are rigorously confined, and energy and material resources are carefully conserved. Guest quarters seem to meet in spontaneous groups among the trees, standing lightly on their footings and linked by a continuous system of decks, walkways, and paths.

This is the sunny eastern side of the Cascades, where mountain scenery meets seasonal extremes of heat and cold. Sheltered under high-peaked, snow-shedding roofs, meeting rooms and guest rooms share a Northwest architectural language adapted from the mountain vernacular. Massing and details are chosen for functional fit with the climate, the sun, and shade. Tall windows in the gable ends of the guest rooms bring visitors into close contact with the filtered light and the rocky scenery surrounding them, and bracketed overhangs protect them as they come and go.

To encourage interaction, living quarters allow for several different levels of enclosure. High ceilings with exposed trusses and bed lofts accommodate one to four guests. All open out to sheltered spaces just outside the door, under generous overhangs supported by heavy angle brackets. Linked by walkways, guest rooms surround intimate courtyards captured from the natural environment. All plantings added to the site are native to the area.

Public facilities include meeting rooms of several scales, an administration building, a dining hall, a conference headquarters building, and a central auditorium. Several of the structures mix new construction with elements of older buildings on the site, including open-air porches and air-lock entries.

In addition to hosting large and small conferences, Sleeping Lady is a retreat for individuals and families. All can use a pool and hot tub built into a rocky shelf in the knoll, just above a center for sauna and massage.

TOP: Sacred place-defining qualities are preserved and celebrated for quiet rejuvenating qualities and concomitant opportunities for quiet reflection.

ABOVE: Seasonally sensitive design welcomes clientele for consistent year-round conference bookings and performance events.

Sleeping Lady is perhaps the largest but lightest layer of construction on a site that has been settled in several waves. The first was the Civilian Conservation Corps, which built a ranger station and nearby ski lodge during the Depression. The barracks and mess hall were revamped as a church camp in the 1940s.

As a youngster, media heiress and environmental activist Harriet Bullitt spent summers near the camp at a family retreat, riding and wandering in the woods. The Catholic diocese decided to divest itself of the property in 1990. To save a regional legacy for future generations, Bullitt bought the camp. Sleeping Lady began with Bullitt's attachment to the place and her desire to set new standards for environmental stewardship and earth-wise accommodations. The design grows naturally from her philosophy, which can be summarized in the environmental dictum: reduce, reuse, recycle.

To begin with, new buildings at Sleeping Lady were kept to areas already disturbed by previous construction. These areas, scattered on the flat ground at the base of the granite knoll, allow natural vegetation to close in around minimal footprints. Invasive plant species were removed, and the previously developed land was reused as building site or garden space, where organic flowers and vegetables are grown.

The sustainable systems of Sleeping Lady were selected and built according to a strict order of priority—beginning with simple, non-engineered solutions and descending to the use of complex technologies.

Some of the original construction was not salvageable. However, most of the small buildings were moved and incorporated into new structures. A chapel built by the diocese for the church camp was reconfigured as the conference plenary and auditorium for the center. An outer lobby now wraps around the stone walls of the original chapel, which is reborn as a stage and auditorium. Salvaged lumber from the local City Hall was used for exposed framing and finish, and exterior decking of recycled plastic was used for walkways and porches. Some of the wood floors are recycled from the original buildings. Bathroom floors are covered with linseed oil and plant fiber Marmoleum. Nearly everything old found a place in the new scheme of things. Old gypsum board, for instance, became a lime supplement for the vegetable garden. Over 85 percent of demolition and construction waste was diverted from the landfill.

Thermal performance begins with a double wall system and insulated structural panel roof assemblies throughout the camp. Cavities are insulated with mastic-cellulose made from ground computer paper and cardboard boxes, blown into the walls with a water-based, fire-retardant binder that is non-toxic. Load-bearing members are held inside the insulated envelope of the walls, which are detailed to reduce thermal bridging.

Most windows are operable. The heating and cooling system is ground-source, digitally controlled and programmed to respond to occupancy and to indoor and outdoor temperatures. Every building is equipped with air-to-air heat recovery ventilation equipment, and waste heat is recovered in the kitchen and laundry to heat water. In a similar order of priority, the effective use of daylighting offsets lighting costs. Compact fluorescents, occupancy sensors, and dimming do their part to keep energy usage down.

The retreat and conference center is not a well-kept secret in the Leavenworth area. To support the local community and its economy, Sleeping Lady was built by local contractors operating under an umbrella company formed by the owner. Their new enthusiasm for adapting new and old construction practices for long-term sustainability is changing the way business is done, just as Sleeping Lady is changing the way people rest, renew their ties, and plan their futures together.

Jones & Jones was master planner, architect, and landscape architect for Sleeping Lady Mountain Retreat for owner Harriet Bullitt.

Timeless style draws heavily from local vernacular building form; simple small building clusters can be added to, easily tailoring development to evolving needs.

Sleeping Lady site plan.

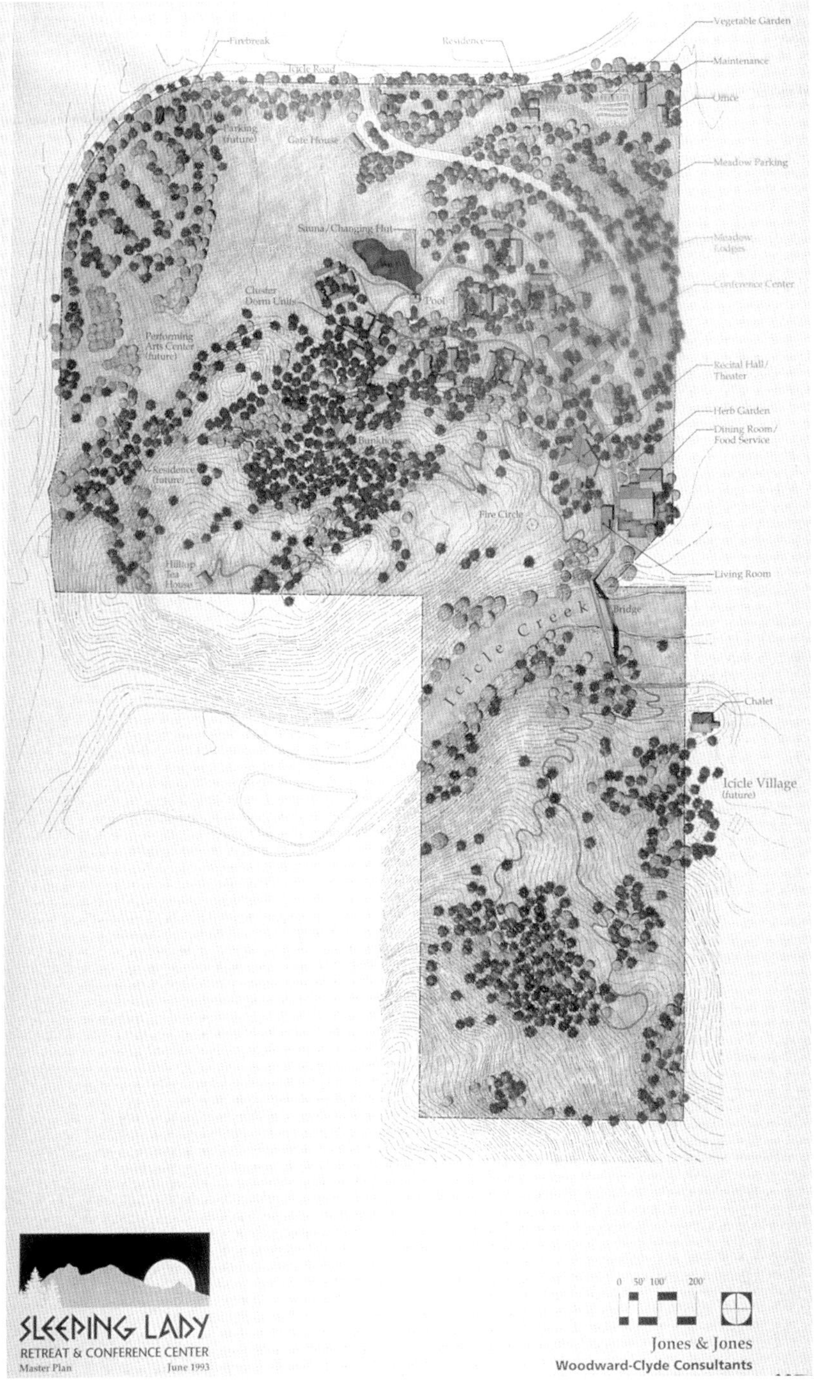

A preliminary master plan preserved a major portion of the site, reused a number of existing buildings, located parking away from the retreat area, clustered buildings, and focused the new development where the site had been previously occupied.

ABOVE: Climate-responsive, place-connected buildings enhance their context and resonate with the innate sensibilities of the users: it feels right, and people return again and again.

RIGHT: At housing clusters, open decks give way to covered porches; guests enjoy morning coffee while viewing marshland birds.

ABOVE: To minimize the built area, aesthetic and flexible space functions alternately for trade shows, as performance lobby, break-out meeting space, and an occasional dance hall.

RIGHT: The quiet presence of nature is enhanced by a unique and carefully designed interface between the site and the conference programs.

ABOVE: A renovated chapel recalls the history of the former CYO camp, and while housing conference plenaries and larger communal performances it moves conferees toward a new vision of our future.

RIGHT: Good local food and gathering daily around the table build a mutually nourishing community.

LEFT: Compact guest rooms can be let as singles, family rooms, or shared successfully, providing accommodations at a variety of income levels.

ABOVE: Renovated existing Civilian Conservation Corps buildings double as small meeting rooms and cozy living spaces.

SELECTED CLIENTS AND PROJECTS

CLIENTS

Institutional

Arizona Sonora Desert Museum
Bergen County Zoological Park
Bill Graham Presents
Boeing Company
Busch Gardens
Caldwell Zoo, Texas
Calgary Zoo, Botanical Garden and Prehistoric Park
Centre City Development Corporation
Chandler Brooks & Donahoe Inc
The Confluence Project
Dallas Arboretum and Botanical Gardens
Dallas Zoological Society
Detroit Zoological Institute
The Evergreen State College
Family Golf Centers Inc
Fifth Avenue Local Improvement District
Flint Horticultural Society
Fred Hutchinson Cancer Research Center
Honolulu Zoo
Jacksonville Zoological Gardens
John Ball Zoological Garden
Living Desert Zoo and Garden State Park
Los Angeles Zoo
National Tropical Botanic Garden
National Trust for Historic Preservation
North Idaho College
Pacific Science Center
Pacifica: A Garden in the Siskiyous
Quail Botanical Gardens Foundation
Riverbanks Zoological Park and Botanical Garden
San Antonio Zoological Society
San Francisco Zoological Society
Santa Barbara Zoo
Seattle Chinese Garden Society
Seattle Public Library
Sleeping Lady Mountain Retreat & Conference Center
Smithsonian Institution
St. Louis Zoological Park
Travelers Hotel Company
Trillium Corporation
Tucson Children's Museum
University of Alaska, Fairbanks
University of British Columbia, Museum of Anthropology
University of North Carolina
University of Oregon
University of Washington
Walt Disney Imagineering
Washington Park Zoo, Portland
Washington State Major League Baseball Stadium
Weyerhaeuser Company
Woodland Park Zoological Society
Zoological Society of Florida
Zoological Society of San Diego

Non-Profit

California Arboretum Foundation
California Wildlife Foundation
Casa Latina, Seattle
Cedar Lake Park Association
El Centro de La Raza, Seattle
Environmental Coalition of South Seattle (ECOSS)
Friends of the Falls
I'm A PAL Foundation

Institute for Community Leadership
Mount Baker Community Club
Mountains to Sound Greenway Trust
The Nature Conservancy, North Central Washington Unit
The Nature Conservancy of Washington
Nisqually River Council
People for Puget Sound
River Foundation
San Juan Preservation Trust
Scenic America
Trust for Public Land
Urban Open Space Foundation
WWII Nikkei Internment and Exclusion Memorial Committee

Municipal

City & County of Honolulu, Hawaii, Parks & Recreation Department
City of Bainbridge Island, Washington, Park & Recreation District
City of Bellevue, Washington, Parks & Community Services
City of Boise, Idaho, Department of Parks & Recreation
City of Bothell, Washington, Department of Community Services
City of Denver, Colorado, Department of Parks
City of Eatonville, Washington, Historic Preservation Commission
City of Ketchikan, Alaska
City of Mount Vernon, Washington
City of Olympia, Washington, Parks & Recreation Department
City of Portland, Oregon, Bureau of Planning
City of Renton, Washington, Parks Division
City of Richland, Washington, Planning Department
City of San Diego, California, Park & Recreation Department
City of SeaTac, Washington, Public Works
City of Seattle, Washington, Department of Community Development
City of Seattle, Washington, Department of Neighborhoods, Historic Preservation
City of Seattle, Washington, Parks & Recreation
City of Skagway, Alaska
City of Spokane, Washington, Parks & Recreation Department
City of Tucson, Arizona, Rio Nuevo Facilities District
City of Vancouver, Washington, Board of Parks & Recreation
City of Yakima, Washington, Parks & Recreation
Minneapolis, Park & Recreation Board, Minnesota
Port of Portland, Oregon
Port of Seattle, Facilities Development & Management, Washington
Richland Public Facilities District, Washington
Seattle City Light
Spokane Valley Chamber of Commerce, Washington
Tacoma Metropolitan Park District, Washington

County

Allegheny County, Pennsylvania
King County Department of Planning & Community Development, Washington
King County Parks, Planning & Resources Department, Washington
King County Wildlife Program, Washington
San Juan County, Washington
Spokane County Parks, Washington
Whatcom County, Washington

State

Kentucky Transportation Cabinet
State of Idaho
State of Montana
State of New Mexico
State of Oregon
State of Washington
Washington Governor's Select Committee on the Columbia River Gorge
Pacific Northwest River Basins Commission

Federal

Atomic Energy Commission
Federal Highway Administration
National Park Service—Alaska Regional Office
National Park Service—Denver Service Center
National Park Service—Idaho
National Park Service—North Cascades National Park
National Park Service—Pacific West Region
National Park Service—Southeast Utah Group
Smithsonian Institution
U.S. Army Corps of Engineers
U.S. Bureau of Land Management
USDA Forest Service

Native American

The Agua Caliente Band of Cahuilla Indians
Chief Seattle Club
The Coeur d'Alene Tribe
The Confederated Tribes of the Grand Ronde
The Confederated Tribes of the Salish & Kootenai
The Confederated Tribes of the Umatilla Indian Reservation
Colville Confederated Tribes
Institute of American Indian Arts
The Kalispel Tribe of Indians
The Makah Tribal Council
The Muckleshoot Indian Tribe
The Pomo Tribal Council
Seattle Indian Health Board
The Snoqualmie Indian Tribe
Southern Ute Cultural Center-Museum
The Spokane Tribe of Indians
Squaxin Island Tribe
United Indians of All Tribes Foundation
The Wampanoag Tribe of Gay Head (Aquinnah)
The Wanapum Tribe
The Zuni Tribe

International

Belize Zoo Tropical Education Center
Grand Park National Zoo, Korea
Dublin Zoo
East Coast National Scenic Area Authority, Taiwan
Forestal Trillium Ltda., Chile
Fundación Mexicana Para La Educacion Ambiental A.C.
Guam Economic Development Authority
Jerusalem Foundation
Jurubena Bertiga International, Malaysia
Northeast Coast Scenic Area Authority, Taiwan
Perth Zoo, Australia
Provincial Government of Québec
Royal Melbourne Zoological Gardens
Seoul National University
Singapore Botanic Gardens
Tokyo Department of Parks & Recreation
Zoologico de Morelia, Mexico
Zoologico de Salta, Argentina

PROJECTS

the 1970s

Chena River Floodway and Landscape Regeneration Plan
Fairbanks, Alaska
Chief Joseph Dam Powerhouse Visitor Facility and Landscape Reconstruction
Bridgeport, Washington
Denny Regrade Development Plan/Open Space Plan
Seattle, Washington
Federal Highway Administration *Aesthetics and Visual Resource Management for Highways*
Washington, DC
Fifth Avenue Boulevard Streetscape
Seattle, Washington
Green River Study, Corridor Plan, and Trail Master Plan
King County, Washington
Interstate 705 Structural Feasibility and Concept Study
Tacoma, Washington
Living Desert Zoological and Botanical State Park Master Plan
Carlsbad, New Mexico
Lower Little Spokane River Suitability Study
Spokane, Washington
Makah De'aht Tribal Elders Center
Neah Bay, Washington
Measuring the Social Attitudes and Aesthetic and Ecological Considerations of Nuclear Power Plant Siting
Battelle Pacific Northwest Laboratries for the Atomic Energy Commission
Newhalem Campground, North Cascades National Park Environmental Assessment
North Cascades National Park, Washington
Nooksack River Plan
Whatcom County, Washington
Northwest Trek Wildlife Park
Eatonville, Washington
Occidental Square
Seattle, Washington
Pioneer Square - "Two Parks for Seattle's Historic District"
Seattle, Washington
Point Defiance Zoo Rocky Shores Exhibit
Tacoma, Washington
Stehekin North Cascades Transportation Plan
North Cascades National Park, Washington
Tennant Lake Interpretive Center and Fragrance Garden
Ferndale, Washington
Tilikum Place
Seattle, Washington
University of Washington - Washington Park Arboretum Master Plan Update
Seattle, Washington
University of Washington - Union Bay Teaching and Research Arboretum Master Plan
Seattle, Washington
Upper Susitna River, Alaska: An Inventory and Evaluation of the Environmental, Aesthetic, and Recreational Resources
Anchorage, Alaska
Visual Impact of High Voltage Transmission Facilities in Northern Idaho and Northwestern Montana
Idaho and Montana
Washington State Scenic and Recreational Highway Study
Washington
Woodland Park Zoo Long Range Master Plan
Seattle, Washington
Woodland Park Zoological Gardens Gorilla Habitat
Seattle, Washington
Yakima River Regional Greenway Master Plan
Yakima, Washington

the 1980s

Belize Zoo Master Plan
Belize
Capitol Lake Heritage Park Renovation Master Plan
Olympia, Washington
Center for Urban Horticulture, Douglas Research Conservatory
University of Washington
Seattle, Washington
Columbia River Gorge Study
Washington/Oregon
Dallas Arboretum and Botanic Garden Master Plan
Dallas, Texas
Eagle Island State Park
Boise, Idaho
El Centro de La Raza Master Plan, José Marti Child Development Center, and Performance Kiosko
Seattle, Washington
Explore Park Master Plan
Roanoke, Virginia
FHWA "Field Guide": Visual Impact Assessment for Highway Projects
Washington, DC
Gene Coulon Memorial Beach Park
Renton, Washington
Honolulu Zoo Children's Learning Center
Honolulu, Hawaii
Honolulu Zoo Master Plan
Honolulu, Hawaii
Los Angeles State and County Arboretum Master Plan
Arcadia, California
Mercer Slough Nature Park
Bellevue, Washington
New Jerusalem Metropolitan Zoo Master Plan
Jerusalem, Israel
Newcastle Beach Park
Bellevue, Washington
Nisqually River Basin Education and Interpretive Enhancement Feasibility Study
Nisqually Basin, Washington
North Carolina Botanical Garden Master Plan
Chapel Hill, North Carolina
North Fork Snoqualmie River Recreational and Aesthetic Resources Study
Washington
Northeast Coast Scenic Area Recreation Master Plan
Yenliao, Fulong Coast, Taiwan
Northwest Alaskan Gas Pipeline Aesthetic Management
Alaska
Point Defiance Zoo Polar Bear and Musk Ox Habitats
Tacoma, Washington
Point Defiance Zoo/Aquarium, Aquarium Renovations
Tacoma, Washington
Portland International Airport Parkway
Portland, Oregon
Roanoke River Greenway Master Plan
Roanoke, Virginia
San Diego Harborfront Open Space Invitational Competition
San Diego, California
San Diego Wild Animal Park African Plains Mini Master Plan
Escondido, California
San Diego Wild Animal Park Bazaar Thorntree Gift Shop Renovation
Escondido, California
San Diego Wild Animal Park Nairobi Village Master Plan
Escondido, California
San Diego Wild Animal Park Rhino Holding
Escondido, California
San Diego Zoo African Rock Kopje Exhibit
San Diego, California
San Diego Zoo Master Plan
San Diego, California
San Diego Zoo Sun Bear Forest
San Diego, California
San Diego Zoo Tiger River Trail/Cascade Canyon
San Diego, California
Travelers/Post Mews Mixed-Use Condominum
Seattle, Washington
Trillium Block Master Plan
Bellingham, Washington
University of Washington - Center for Urban Horticulture
Seattle, Washington
University of Washington - South Campus Urban Design Study and Southwest Campus Planning Study
Seattle, Washington
Woodland Park Zoological Gardens African Savanna
Seattle, Washington
Woodland Park Zoological Gardens Elephant Forest Exhibit
Seattle, Washington

the 1990s

"A Walk on the Mountain" Pedestrian Bridge/Waterfront Park
Tacoma, Washington
Alaska Square Park
Seattle, Washington
Aquinnah Cultural Center Master Plan
Martha's Vineyard, Massachussetts
Arizona Sonora Desert Museum Grasslands Exhibit
Tucson, Arizona
Bellevue Parks Interpretive Plan
Bellevue, Washington
Bering Land Bridge National Preserve Concept Plan and Environmental Impact Statement
Nome, Alaska
Boeing North Duwamish Waterway Campus IASL (Integrated Aircraft Systems Laboratory)
Seattle, Washington
Busch Gardens Myombe Reserve
Tampa, Florida
Cedar Lake Park and Trail (with Richard Haag)
Minneapolis, Minnesota
Central Waterfront Project
Seattle, Washington

Cheju Island Nature and Culture-Based Tourism Plan
Cheju Island, Korea
Dallas Zoo Gorilla Research Station (Jake L. Hamon Gorilla Conservation Research Center)
Dallas, Texas
Disney's Animal Kingdom: Kilimanjaro Safari, Maharajah Jungle Trek, and Pagani Forest Exploration Trail
Orlando, Florida
Duwamish River Gateway Parks
Seattle, Washington
Elwha River Ecosystem Restoration
Olympic Peninsula, Washington
The Evergreen State College Longhouse Education and Cultural Center
Olympia, Washington
Fort Vancouver National Historic Reserve Feasibility Study and EIS
Vancouver, Washington
Fred Hutchinson Cancer Research Center Landscape Design
Seattle, Washington
Green Island Ecotourism Master Plan
Green Island, Taiwan
Guam Territorial Aquarium Plan
Guam
Honolulu Zoo Savanna
Honolulu, Hawaii
Houston Zoological Gardens Master Plan
Houston, Texas
Institute of American Indian Art Planning & Design
Santa Fe, New Mexico
Interbay Family Golf Club and Clubhouse
Seattle, Washington
Jardin Xochitla Nature Reserve and Botanical Gardens Master Plan
Tepotzotlán, Mexico
Ketchikan Civic Center
Ketchikan, Alaska
Klondike Goldrush National Historic Park Master Plan
Skagway, Alaska
Mountains to Sound Greenway Plan for the Mountains to Sound Greenway Trust
Washington
Nez Perce National Historical Park General Management Plan
Spalding, Idaho
Nisqually River Basin Interpretive Center Concept Development
Nisqually Basin, Washington
Oregon Coast Highway 101 Scenic Byway
Oregon
Paradise Ski Dorm
Paradise, Washington
Perth Zoo Master Plan and East African Savanna Exhibit
Perth, Australia
Pittsburgh International Airport Three Rivers Parkway Design Charette
Pittsburgh, Pennsylvania
Putrajaya Botanic Gardens Master Plan
Kuala Lumpur
Québec Ecological Park Master Plan
Québec City, Québec
Renton Waterworks Garden (with Lorna Jordan, Artist)
Renton, Washington
Rio Condor Sustainable Forest Development Plan
Tierra del Fuego, Chile
Safeco Field Urban Design and Streetscape
Seattle, Washington
San Antonio Zoo Master Plan
San Antonio, Texas
San Diego Wild Animal Park Long Range Plan
Escondido, California
San Diego Zoo Gorilla Tropics Exhibit
San Diego, California
San Diego Zoo Treehouse, Restaurants, Gift Shop, and Events Center
San Diego, California
San Juan County Open Space and Conservation Plan
Friday Harbor, Washington
Seattle Chinese Garden
Seattle, Washington
Singapore Botanic Gardens Redevelopment Master Plan
Singapore
Sleeping Lady Retreat and Conference Center
Leavenworth, Washington
Southeast Alaska Visitors Information Center, USDA Forest Service (with Charles Bettisworth & Company Inc.)
Ketchikan, Alaska
Spokane River Centennial Trail Master Plan
Spokane, Washington
Spokane Tribe Cultural Learning Center
Wellpinit, Washington
St. Louis Zoo "The River's Edge" Exhibits
St. Louis, Missouri
St. Louis Zoo Vision Plan
St. Louis, Missouri
Tepotzotlán Historic Center Ecological Rescue Plan (Plan Ecatl)
Tepotzotlán, Mexico
Washington State Capitol Campus Master Plan
Olympia, Washington
Washington State Ecotourism Strategy
Washington
Weyerhaeuser Forest Aesthetics Workshops
Tacoma, Washington
White River Amphitheater Landscape and Site Development
Auburn, Washington
Yosemite Cultural Landscape Study, Pre-Development Concept Plan, and Development Concept Plan
Yosemite Valley, California

the 2000s

Agua Caliente Cultural Museum
Palm Springs, California
Arroyo Seco Parkway Vision Plan
Pasadena, California
Balboa Park Master Plan
San Diego, California
Bosque Redondo Memorial and Visitor Center
Sante Fe, New Mexico
Cascade Neighborhood Center EcoRenovation Plan
Seattle, Washington
Cedar River Watershed Education Center
Cedar Falls, Washington
Cesar Chavez Park
Seattle, Washington
Chief Seattle Club—Monterey Hotel Restoration
Seattle, Washington
Columbia River Confluence Project
Vancouver, Washington
Commons Park (with Civitas, Inc.)
Denver, Colorado
Confluence Project: Vancouver Land Bridge
Vancouver, Washington
Detroit Zoo Arctic Ring of Life
Royal Oak, Michigan
Detroit Zoo Master Plan
Royal Oak, Michigan
Detroit Zoo National Amphibian Conservation Center
Royal Oak, Michigan
Dublin Zoo Asian Elephants
Dublin, Ireland
Duwamish Riverfront Revival Plan for the Environmental Coalition of South Seattle (ECOSS) (with Anchor Environmental)
Seattle, Washington
Ebey's Landing National Historic Reserve Cultural Landscape and General Management Plan (with the National Park Service)
Whidbey Island, Washington
Fairgrounds Community Park
Vancouver, Washington
Fort Vancouver Concept Plan and Cultural Landscape Report
Vancouver, Washington
Grand Ronde Museum and Cultural Master Plan
Grand Ronde, Oregon
Great Spokane River Gorge Strategic Master Plan
Spokane, Washington
Greenprint for King County—King County Land Acquisition Strategy
Washington
Hanford Reach National Monument Heritage Visitors Center
Richland, Washington
Hill Slough "Pacific Flyway Museum" Conceptual Interpretive Plan
Suisun Bay, California
Ice Age Floods Interpretive Plan and Alternatives Study
Montana, Idaho, Washington, and Oregon
Icicle Creek Music Center
Leavenworth, Washington
The Jack Hunter O'Dell Reflection and Education Center Concept Plan
Kent, Washington
Jacksonville Zoo Giraffe Savanna Exhibit (with Gresham Smith & Partners)
Jacksonville, Florida
John Ball Zoo Mokomboso Valley
Grand Rapids, Michigan
Kalispel Tribe Interpretive Center
Usk, Washington
Living Desert Zoological and Botanical State Park Bobcat/Mountain Lion Exhibit
Carlsbad, New Mexico
Living Desert Zoological and Botanical State Park Nocturnal House
Carlsbad, New Mexico
Los Angeles Zoo Campo Gorilla Reserve
Los Angeles, California
Los Angeles Zoo Veterinary Facility
Los Angeles, California

Madison Central Park "Community Visioning" Process and Planning
Madison, Wisconsin
Melbourne Zoo Master Plan
Parkville, Victoria, Australia
Melbourne Zoo Trail of the Elephants
Melbourne, Australia
Mercer Slough Environmental Education Center
Bellevue, Washington
Miami Metrozoo "Tropical America" Exhibit
Miami, Florida
Minidoka Internment National Monument General Management Plan
Hagerman, Idaho
Mt. Baker Ridge Viewpoint
Seattle, Washington
National Museum of the American Indian on the Mall
Washington, DC
National Tropical Botanic Garden Master Plan
Kauai, Hawaii
Nez Perce National Historical Park General Management Plan
Idaho, Montana, Oregon, and Washington
Nikkei World War II Exclusion Memorial—"Nidoto Nai Yoni/Let It Not Happen Again"
Bainbridge Island, Washington
North Idaho College/Coeur d'Alene Tribe Longhouse Conceptual Design
Coeur d'Alene, Idaho
North SeaTac Park
SeaTac, Washington
Oxbow Park
Seattle, Washington
Pacific Flyway Discovery Center at Gray Lodge Wildlife Refuge
Gridley, California
Paris Lexington Road
Lexington, Kentucky
People's Lodge
Seattle, Washington
Rattlesnake Lake Recreation Area Study
Cedar Falls, Washington
Ravalli Hill Interpretive Overlook Concept Design
Ravalli Hill, Montana
Rio Nuevo Cultural Facilities District Master Plan
Tucson, Arizona
Sacajawea State Park Preliminary Design Concept
Washington
San Antonio Zoo Africa Live
San Antonio, Texas
San Diego River Park Master Plan
San Diego, California
San Diego Wild Animal Park Condor Ridge
Escondido, California
San Francisco Zoo Children's Zoo Meerkat/Prairie Dogs Exhibit
San Francisco, California
San Francisco Zoo Lemur Forest and Primate Discovery Center
San Francisco, California
Seattle Central Library Urban Design and Streetscape
Seattle, Washington
Seattle Chinese Garden
Seattle, Washington
Seoul Grand Park Zoo Master Plan
Seoul, Korea
Snoqualmie Point Scenic View Park Master Site Concept Plan
Snoqualmie, Washington
Southern Ute Museum and Cultural Center
Ignacio, Colorado
Spokane Tribe Urban Cultural Center at *Snweymn*
Spokane, Washington
Two Sisters Return: Snoqualmie Welcome Center
Snoqualmie, Washington
U.S. 93 Highway Design
Evaro to Polson, Montana
Umatilla Tribe Headquarters Master Plan
Pendleton, Oregon
Umatilla Tribe Public Safety Building
Pendleton, Oregon
University of Oregon Many Nations Longhouse
Eugene, Oregon
University of Washington Tacoma Campus Master Plan (with LMN Architects)
Tacoma, Washington
Vancouver National Historic Reserve Cultural Landscape Report
Vancouver, Washington
Washington Coastal Corridor Scenic Byway Master Plan (Highway 101)
Washington
Zuni A:shiwi Cultural and Arts Center
Zuni Pueblo, New Mexico

PHOTOGRAPHY AND SKETCHES CREDITS

Civitas, Inc.: p 23 above right, bottom

Katherine Fogden: p 59, p 61

Adam Jones: p 31, p 33, p 34 above left and below, pp 35–37, p 63

Kaija Jones: jacket photograph of Jones & Jones Principals

Robert C. Lautman: p 53 above, p 56 below right, p 57 below right

National Museum of the American Indian: p 56 above left and below left

Peter Sackett: jacket photograph of Clair Enlow

Seth Seablom: p 69, p 71 center, p 72 above left

Dan Williams: p 71 below left and below right

Michael Ian Shopenn: p 75, pp 78–83

Lara Swimmer: cover, p 12 below, pp 13–19

Other photography and illustrations by Jones & Jones